COMING OF
POLITICAL AGE

COMING OF POLITICAL AGE

American Schools and the
Civic Development of
Immigrant Youth

Rebecca M. Callahan and
Chandra Muller

Russell Sage Foundation • New York

The Russell Sage Foundation

The Russell Sage Foundation, one of the oldest of America's general purpose foundations, was established in 1907 by Mrs. Margaret Olivia Sage for "the improvement of social and living conditions in the United States." The Foundation seeks to fulfill this mandate by fostering the development and dissemination of knowledge about the country's political, social, and economic problems. While the Foundation endeavors to assure the accuracy and objectivity of each book it publishes, the conclusions and interpretations in Russell Sage Foundation publications are those of the authors and not of the Foundation, its Trustees, or its staff. Publication by Russell Sage, therefore, does not imply Foundation endorsement.

Library of Congress Cataloging-in-Publication Data

Callahan, Rebecca.
    Coming of political age : American schools and the civic development of immigrant youth / Rebecca Callahan and Chandra L. Muller.
        pages cm
Includes bibliographical references and index.
    ISBN 978-0-87154-578-7 (pb : alk. paper) — ISBN 978-1-61044-794-2 (ebook)
1. Children of immigrants—Education—United States.   2. Children of immigrants—Political activity—United States.   3. Community development—United States.   I. Title.
    LC3731.C3316 2013
    371.826'9120973—dc23   2012046069

Text design by Suzanne Nichols.

RUSSELL SAGE FOUNDATION
112 East 64th Street, New York, New York 10065
10 9 8 7 6 5 4 3 2 1

CONTENTS

FIGURES AND TABLES

ABOUT THE AUTHORS

REBECCA M. CALLAHAN is assistant professor of curriculum and instruction and a faculty research affiliate at the Population Research Center at the University of Texas at Austin.

CHANDRA MULLER is professor of sociology and a faculty research affiliate at the Population Research Center at the University of Texas at Austin.

MOLLY DONDERO is a graduate student in sociology and a research trainee at the Population Research Center at the University of Texas at Austin.

ACKNOWLEDGMENTS

The ideas for this study were first articulated and fleshed out during a series of walks around Town Lake in Austin just south of the Texas state capitol, later named in honor of Lady Bird Johnson and her work for the community. Later, we solidified the plans on a walk around the grounds of the 9/11 Monument in Washington, D.C. Although these walks involved significant symbolic backdrops for our study—Texas was in the process of becoming a Latino-majority state as the politicians at the state capitol are keenly aware, and our nation's understanding of global issues and peoples were transformed at the turn of this century—we were pondering the implications of our work on immigrant high school students' course-taking.

When we first joined forces, Rebecca Callahan had come to work with Chandra Muller on her Adolescent Health and Academic Achievement (AHAA) project (funded by the National Institute of Child Health and Human Development (NICHD R01 HD40428-02S1) and the National Science Foundation (HRD-0523046). The study was investigating how education and the high school context shaped adolescents' transition to adulthood. The project focuses on the use of high school transcripts to quantify students' experiences in academic subjects. Callahan had a background in English language learners and English as a Second Language (ESL) issues and with the support of an American Educational Research Association/Institute of Education Services (AERA-IES) post-doctoral fellowship led a component of the AHAA that used high school course-taking records to understand the experiences of English language learners. Drawing on our individual areas of expertise in this early collaboration, we developed a series of studies exploring the processing of immigrant, language minority students in U.S. high schools. This early collaboration was instrumental to our present work as it allowed us to investigate how schools processed immigrant, language minority students relative to their native-born, native-English-speaking peers.

Following our collaborative work investigating the academic experiences of children of immigrant parents, we were eager to consider other aspects of the high school experience. Muller brought a focus on civic development to the table, and Callahan an interest in immigrant incorporation. As a K-12 educator, Callahan observed firsthand the engagement of immigrant youth in the social world of the high school. Her work as a teacher suggested students' formal and informal school experiences might play differently based on parental nativity. These early discussions just south of the capitol brought us to consider the *other* aspect of schools and schooling in the United States, the civic development of youth.

Specifically, we began to ask how high schools might prepare children of immigrants for citizenship in young adulthood. Muller's expertise in school context and the math and science pipeline, combined with Callahan's linguistic focus, allowed us to question whether and how children of immigrants might interact with different school and community contexts to engage as young adults in the civic lives of their communities. The Add Health/AHAA dataset with its early adulthood indicators was perfectly poised to allow us to ask and answer these questions. We are deeply indebted to the Russell Sage Foundation for the opportunity to pursue this line of inquiry (RSF Grant #: 88-06-12; *The Roles of Language and Education in Adolescent Immigrants' Civic Integration during the Transition to Adulthood)*. Specifically, we would like to thank Suzanne Nichols for her consistent, clear support and encouragement throughout this project, Eric Wanner, president of the Russell Sage Foundation, Aixa Cintrón-Velez, our initial program officer, the Russell Sage grants board, and the very patient and diligent editors, Cindy Buck and Jean Blackburn.

The *Language and Education* study built on prior research exploring issues of assimilation—language in particular and family in general—and school context. To our surprise, however, our preliminary civic models produced largely null effects. Although the literature on immigrant adults' civic engagement highlights the importance of the home language in access to information, the same pattern did not hold true among adolescents. Primary language use relates to achievement and course-taking among immigrant youth, with little to no association with civic and political behaviors during early adulthood. Similarly, extracurricular involvement and volunteering shapes adolescents' social experiences, but does so for all adolescents, regardless of parental nativity. Instead, our findings suggested that high school social studies in particular may influence the civic and political behaviors of children of immigrants in a way it does not for their native-born peers. Our early collaborative work on course-taking allowed us to isolate students' social studies experiences in their overall educational profile. Ultimately, we found that community does matter, but it matters in a different way than we expected.

This book expands on the specific social studies mechanisms that foster immigrant students' civic development.

In general, the work in these pages reflects a true collaboration, and one where both authors contributed equally. The exception is the complementary qualitative study, *New Citizens in a New Century,* developed and carried out by Callahan. Through the generous support of the Russell Sage Foundation, Callahan interviewed high school social studies teachers from across the country and their former students, now Latino/a young adults. In these interviews, Callahan and her research assistant spoke to teachers about their perceptions of immigrant youth and their expectations for them. These interviews proved central for understanding our quantitative results. The support and cooperation of these teachers and their former students provided a depth and richness to our work, and we are grateful to them all for taking the time to give us such valuable insights. In addition, Callahan would like to extend her appreciation not only to anonymous reviewers of the initial proposal who helped to shape it into a rich, challenging study, but also to her colleagues Linda Harklau and Kathryn Obenchain. Dr. Harklau offered considerable methodological support and insight in the early stages of study design and data collection. Dr. Obenchain shared her expertise in social studies classroom and curricular research in shaping supplemental analyses of the data. Allen Lynn, while a graduate assistant at the University of Georgia, also assisted Callahan with the initial data collection and transcription processes. We appreciate the suggestions of an anonymous reviewer of this book who urged us to incorporate more of the interview data throughout the narrative. Doing so allowed us to forefront the voices of the teachers and, most importantly, their former students as they transitioned into adult civic society.

Although our collaborative relationship has evolved since we first began working together, from mentor and mentee to peers, we owe a debt of gratitude to many other people and organizations who have supported us along the way. We have carried out the bulk of our work at The University of Texas Population Research Center (NIH 5 R24 HD042849). The Population Research Center NIH training center grant (5 T32 HD007081) provided invaluable assistance by supporting several graduate students who assisted us. Molly Dondero's work was critical to the development of the first chapter. Lindsey Wilkinson, who is now on the faculty at Oregon State University, made several critical contributions to our early work exploring linguistic stratification in high schools. The articles that we coauthored with her, along with some additional analyses that she provided, were crucial to the evolution of this book. In addition, we are thankful to Kathryn Schiller for her collaboration and considerable methodological input throughout the process. And, this would not have been possible without our talented and resourceful graduate research assistants in the Population Research Center: Sarah Blanchard,

Melissa Humphries, and Kathryn Henderson; without their valuable help this book would not have been possible. In particular, Humphreys, Muller, and Schiller's forthcoming work contributed to our understanding of the political identities of children of immigrants. Throughout the process, we benefited greatly from the instrumental support and feedback of our colleagues on the twenty-third floor of the University of Texas Population Research Center, especially Kelly Raley, Catherine Riegle-Crumb, and Keith Robinson. The director of the Population Research Center, Mark Hayward, as well as the talented and invaluable administrative and network support staff have been invaluable throughout this process.

In addition to our local colleagues, our earliest collaborations would not have been possible without the support of Felice Levine and the AERA-IES Post-doctoral grants committee. We would have been unable to complete this work without the support and substantive insights of our National Science Foundation program officers as well, Mark Leddy and Larry Suter. Likewise, no great idea goes unchallenged by the keen eye of a journal's editors and reviewers. We would also like to thank the many journal editors along the way who have shepherded our work forward, taking the time to challenge us further. One editor stands out as having been especially influential; Drew Gitomer, former editor of *Educational Evaluation and Policy Analysis,* helped us to recognize the difference of the estimated effect of ESL placement among immigrant students—distinguishing the most recent immigrants who benefitted from the ESL support services from their more English-proficient peers who had been schooled primarily in the United States. And, of course, we are thankful to countless anonymous reviewers along the way who provided considerable feedback and expertise, helping us to solidify and clarify our argument.

And, finally, we extend special thanks to our families for their support, patience, and encouragement as we developed this study at work, on many weekends, over the phone, at coffee houses, and on many walks around town. Bill, Amalia, and Chiara; Andrew, Ryder, and Vito—we thank you for supporting us.

As we continue in our journey, from the trail around Lady Bird Lake to the grounds near our nation's capitol, we see the promising faces of the future. In front of us we see the children of immigrant parents who come to build a stronger, sounder, more hopeful nation.

Rebecca M. Callahan and Chandra Muller

INTRODUCTION

High Schools and the Future of Our Democracy

The whole point of social science in high school [for immigrant children] really . . . is to get these kids to citizenship. What do they really need to know? And so the focus is on democracy and how every vote counts. That's why we set it up that way, to be more involved in their local governments.

—Mr. Schroeder,[1] world history teacher, San Diego

The simple act of voting gives voice to the needs and desires of a population and is a critical aspect of political participation and civic engagement. Voting offers a measure of citizens' perceived agency in society. As a citizenry grows and changes, the political processes associated with its governance are expected to respond in kind. In the American democracy, this relationship requires an educated populace—a citizenry able to recognize and define not only the individual's obligations to the greater society but also the government's obligations to the citizen and to the society at large. American public schools have evolved to address this critical need; through social science instruction, schools educate youth for citizenship and prepare them for political participation. In this book, we unpack the role of social science instruction in the political coming of age of American youth, focusing on the children of immigrants in particular.

Historically, U.S. public schools have been tasked with the preparation of youth for citizenship and participation in the democratic process (Cremin 1951; Goodlad 1984; Marshall 1950). Schools' role in the political preparation of American youth is relevant in the context of our current political discourse across several levels. First, social science instruction is designed to develop a democratic citizenry—that is, a citizenry that shapes its own governance. Second, the civic side of schooling may be particularly salient for children of immigrants who are coming of age in a political system in which their parents are novices as well. Third, the political preparation of children of immigrants increases in importance as the population itself grows, both in the present and into the future. And finally, schools now play these roles in the political preparation of students in an era of unprecedented school accountability. Under the No Child Left Behind Act of 2001 (NCLB) (U.S. Department of Education 2001) and the Obama administration's Race to the Top program initiated in 2009, the ever-increasing pressure on educators and schools to focus on the content areas being tested often leads them to deemphasize the social science curriculum in the process.

The importance of the children of immigrants population to the future of our democracy will only increase in the coming decades, as the population is expected to grow at an unprecedented rate. This book reflects on the relationship between social science instruction and political participation among this expanding population. This relationship may prove particularly sensitive to the well-documented academic and social stratification in U.S. high schools, but here we tease social science instruction apart from the larger scope of overall academic preparation and training. Today, as schools struggle to meet federally imposed accountability measures that indirectly curtail access to social science instruction, the relationship of social science instruction to the civic and political development of children of immigrants may be especially important.

Schools and Citizenship

As our nation faces a heated debate over immigration and immigrant rights, we focus on one critical component of the schools' role in the development of civic engagement—electoral engagement (Keeter, Andolina, and Jenkins 2002)—and on the ways in which schools shape the political participation of young people as they gain the right to vote. In order for our democracy to survive, much less thrive, high schools must prepare students to be active citizens as well as provide them with the skills that they will need for the workforce. Citizenship development requires a sense of commitment, beyond self-interest, to a larger community (Sherrod, Flanagan, and Youniss 2002). The civic education received by American youth shapes the future of our democracy, and among children of immigrants civic education may in fact hold even greater sway. Children of immigrants encounter the social science curriculum with a perspective distinct from those of their peers and their parents. The work presented here attempts to better understand the strengths and characteristics of the perspectives of all youth, and of children of immigrants in particular.

SOCIAL SCIENCE INSTRUCTION: PEDAGOGY, CONTENT, COURSE-TAKING, AND OUTPUTS

The early twentieth century was marked by rapid industrialization and the rise of the urban center as an immigrant receiving ground. During this period, the role of the school in transforming children of immigrants into American citizens grew in importance (Tyack 1974). A century later, U.S. schools remain the primary source of civic preparation, even during recent eras of accountability focused on math and reading. It is not only through direct social science instruction about civic life and democracy but also through language instruction and academic preparation that youth prepare to engage in adult civic society. As schools prepare this next generation of citizens for higher education and jobs, they develop the connections to social institutions—first to school and then to work—that they will carry into their adult lives. Adolescent students receive this academic and social preparation at a critical point in the life course, the transition into young adulthood. The high school is thus well positioned to shape that crucial transition, which defines an individual's contribution not only to the labor force but also to our democracy.

Critics have argued that the dominant pedagogical model in the social sciences, transmission, focuses on the recitation of facts rather than on the development of critical thinking skills (Thornton 1994). Nevertheless, the social science classroom is often held up as a rich context for the development of critical thinking and inquiry through its focus on the development of civic society (Newstreet 2008; ten Dam and Volman 2004). Given its focus on the development and growth of human communities and on patterns of social dominance and renewal, the social science classroom lends itself to the development of students' ability to question a premise, construct an argument, predict its outcome, and debate its merits.

Social science instruction is shaped not only through teachers' pedagogical practices but also through the content of the curriculum. The curricular content of the social science classroom offers the opportunity for students to develop political and civic arguments firsthand, although the social science curriculum has traditionally focused more narrowly on the development of linear history and the impact of geography. So deep is this tradition, in fact, that schools and teachers, as Stephen Thornton (1994) points out, are relatively unwilling to adopt seemingly controversial curriculum in the social sciences. Done well, the study of governments and governance can lead to questioning of the existing political hierarchy. Consciously or not, as Diane Ravitch (2010) has argued, educators may feel pressure from politicians and policymakers not to instill in students the desire to question authority.

Content is determined in part by course sequencing, and the sequence and structure of social science course-taking have remained largely unchanged over the past century: civics or world cultures is generally taught in ninth grade, world and U.S. history in tenth and eleventh grade, and government in twelfth grade (Ross 1997). Richard Niemi and Julia Smith (2001) find that more specialized classes—such as international relations, economics, sociology, or psychology—tend to be offered to students in the later years of

high school, generally after they have fulfilled the base graduation requirements. Such patterns suggest that enrollment in social science coursework
above and beyond high school graduation requirements may distinguish the
students preparing for college from those focused solely on high school graduation.

The quality of social science instruction can be measured by outputs as
diverse as grades, credit accumulation, and—further removed—political participation. Each measure gauges one or more aspects of youths' civic development. To successfully prepare the next wave of citizens, educators in U.S.
high schools must simultaneously develop students' desire to become involved in the community and desire to participate in the political process,
both elements of civic engagement and citizenship (Delli Carpini and Keeter
1997). This can be done through engaging social science pedagogy, content,
and course offerings. Ultimately, successful social science programs will produce engaged citizens, but along the way more proximate measures of effective instruction, such as grades and course-taking, can be used to gauge the
quality of those programs.

DEFINING THE CONTENT OF THE SOCIAL SCIENCE
CURRICULUM: A HISTORY IN CONFLICT

Ideally, the teaching of history and social science is a nonpartisan affair that
allows educators to focus on developing students' ability to critique social
movements, policies, and revolutions, recognize the positions of the actors,
and understand the short- and long-term impacts of these actors and events
on society as a whole. In reality, however, ample evidence points to the content of the social science curriculum being shaped by the political maneuver-
ing of policymakers rather than by educators. Ravitch (2010), for example,
details the vicious political attacks levied by Lynne V. Cheney against the national social studies standards and the federal government's response—under
both Bill Clinton and George W. Bush—distancing itself from the very concept of national standards. Ravitch argues that states were motivated by this
federal social studies standards debacle to produce relatively weak state-level
social studies standards that make little specific mention of history or civic
development. In Texas (where both authors reside), the state social studies
standards were recently revised to increase the number of references to reli-
gion and capitalism and to delete any references to Thomas Jefferson, a pro-
ponent of the separation of church and state. Critics argue that the new standards have produced a laundry list to memorize and leave little room for the
development of critical thinking skills. The dilution of state social studies
standards nationwide serves only to weaken the civic function of school during an era of accountability that is increasingly focused on basic math and
literacy skills.

With the onset of the accountability era, especially the federal No Child

Left Behind (NCLB) mandate passed in 2001, educators have been pressured to focus increasing amounts of time on the tested content areas (Jennings and Renter 2006). Initial reports warned of a decrease in, if not elimination of, classes in physical education, music, and art (Grey 2009; National Education Association 2004; Vincent 2004–2005) as schools implemented three-hour instructional blocks dedicated to the development of isolated reading and math skills. Soon researchers began to document the deemphasis of social science and science in elementary grade classrooms nationwide (Bailey, Shaw, and Hollifield 2006; VanFossen 2005), even as middle and high school teachers were faced with increasing numbers of students who had little preparation in these areas. The year 2007 saw the inclusion of science in the NCLB standards, but social science has yet to be similarly integrated. In fact, some social science educators have argued that increased attention from NCLB would not necessarily benefit their programs (Burroughs, Groce, and Webeck 2005); both district- and state-level accountability systems, they point out, exert sufficient pressure to include social science. The era of accountability has not left social science untouched; indeed, it remains a direct threat to the quality and quantity of social science instruction that students experience in U.S. high schools.

Immigrant Youth, Schools, and Civic Society

Immigrant and language minority youth make up a growing proportion of the American young adult population (Passel and Cohn 2008). For the purposes of our work, we use the terms "immigrant youth" and "children of immigrants" to refer to this rapidly growing population of youth born abroad or in the United States who have at least one foreign-born parent. We consider adolescents born abroad to one or two foreign-born parents to be "first-generation" and those born in the United States to one or two foreign-born parents to be "second-generation." Thus, all remaining youth born in the United States to two native-born parents are "third-plus-generation." At times we distinguish students by generational status, but for the most part we follow in the footsteps of scholars such as Grace Kao and Marta Tienda (1995), who consider having foreign-born parents in the home to be the defining feature of immigrant students' interactions with the school system. As a result, our analyses primarily consider first- and second-generation youth together as they experience and interact with the U.S. school system, developing their civic voice.

How immigrant young adults choose to participate in the political and civic life of the country is likely to have an impact on the civic face of the nation in the future. Language policy in American education focuses on the academic preparation of language minority youth learning English, especially on their academic achievement at grade level.[2] Language policy and planning theorists have long called for greater attention to the civic and political development of immigrant communities through schools and schooling (Horn-berger 2006; McGroarty 2002). Pointing to the growing language minority population of immigrants and the tendency of this population to be under-represented in the polls, they stress the civic role of schooling in the discourse surrounding the education of children of immigrants. We take this school of thought one step further and delve into the civic purposes of the high school social science preparation of our youth.

The core mission of this book is to understand the relationship between adolescents' high school experiences and their political participation as young adults, paying particular attention to children of immigrants. In exploring how schools contribute to civic society through the political development and civic engagement of youth, we recognize that civic engagement is not limited to political engagement (Brady, Verba, and Schlozman 1995) and can pertain more broadly to the interaction of the individual with the larger com-munity and community institutions in the form of volunteering, fund-raising, spending time in religious endeavors, and so on.

Contemporary public schools and their districts offer diverse academic opportunities to students. Schools and districts vary in size (both the number of students served and the number of schools within a local educational agency), student body composition (proportion minority, immigrant, free and reduced lunch, and so on), and funding and available resources and ser-vices, as well as in many other features that may have an impact on the qual-ity of the education that students receive. It is important to remember that not only do schools vary in quality and caliber, but also that children of im-migrants tend to be clustered in relatively poor, urban, high-minority schools. Our analyses take school context into account whenever possible, recogniz-ing its unique role in shaping students' educational experiences and out-comes.

Beyond their composition, resources, and services, American high schools today are more diverse in their course offerings and social organization than these broad indicators reflect (Frank et al. 2008). However, our communities and schools, including the schools attended by the children of immigrants, are also more socioeconomically stratified than ever before. We are well aware that, in contrast to previous eras, educational attainment is vital to economic success and security in today's world, and we bring that awareness to bear on our analysis of the schools attended by the children of immigrants.

CONSIDERING THE FUNCTION OF SCHOOLS: THE POLITICAL OUTCOMES OF IMMIGRANT YOUTH

After the American common school emerged in the midnineteenth century as a means by which to prepare and educate the citizenry for participation in a democratic society, public schooling expanded greatly in response to the influx of immigrants from Europe at the start of the twentieth century (Ty-ack 1974). The common school's emergence brought with it a tension be-tween academically preparing youth to fill jobs and develop skills, on the one hand, and training them in civic engagement and political participation, on the other. Ideally, an effective school produces individuals who are academi-cally *and* politically well prepared; however, educational policies and political pressures in our own era of accountability may shift the balance in our schools—away from their civic goals and toward greater focus on academic goals. We argue that the civic goals of schools are relevant to all students and that they are particularly critical for children of immigrants, whose parents may be relatively less familiar with the U.S. political system.

Over the past century, schools have served as a social and educational nexus in the community where children of immigrants come for socialization into the American mainstream (Olsen 1997). The dramatic increase in the number of children of immigrants among the student population over the past decade has brought new urgency to the role of schools in preparing stu-dents for the democratic process. Today, with the immigrant dispersion into new destinations in the rural and suburban Midwest and Southeast, many schools must address the academic, linguistic, and educational needs of chil-dren of immigrants for the first time, in preparation not only for higher edu-cation and work but for citizenship.

Although we have a relatively thorough understanding of the academic achievement of children of immigrants, particularly in traditional receiving areas, we know much less about their experiences in school or the effects of school on other aspects of their lives. Thus, not only must immigrant-receiving schools address the formal education of children of immigrants, as measured by their math, science, and social science course-taking, but these schools must recognize that they are the social fabric into which young new immigrants are integrated. And with the rapid changes in immigrant demo-graphics, it is more important than ever before to develop our understanding of the experiences in school of children of immigrants and the impact of those experiences on their futures and on the future of our nation. For in-stance, what are the implications of the transformation of the immigrant population in U.S. schools for higher education and for the labor force? What is the impact of this transformation on the social integration of chil-dren of immigrants into the adolescent community? The school experiences of children of immigrants include formal and informal processes, relation-ships, and connections that provide important clues about their political de-velopment and future civic engagement, and our study explores political par-ticipation as an end product of these school experiences during the formative years of adolescence.

Although we certainly acknowledge that individual attributes and family background play important roles in shaping the political participation of young adults, we focus primarily on schools as the primary site of the institutional and social integration of immigrant youth and as an aspect of their lives that can be altered to affect change. Education policy consumes a sizable share of public domestic spending and represents our largest public investment in children and their socialization. As such, the political socialization that takes place in schools is a core mission of the educational system in which we have so heavily invested, and one that may be especially valuable for children of immigrants.

Central Hypotheses

Our first hypothesis is that high school provides an excellent arena for understanding a school's contribution to the political development of children of immigrants. For the majority of adolescent students, high school provides valuable learning opportunities. It has a rich social environment in which young people's identities develop, behavioral norms are conveyed, and information about opportunity and responsibility is shared among students of different backgrounds and social origins. All of these functions foster a connection to the school and are important factors in adolescents' socio-emotional development. The high school also provides formal opportunities to learn, through coursework and other academic activities. These learning opportunities and the stratification that is characteristic of the high school curriculum not only lead to differential postsecondary attainment and labor force opportunities but also affect the social science instruction that takes place.

As many others have argued, we also hypothesize that each aspect of school and schooling—the academic, the civic, and the social—promotes political engagement in early adulthood. Academic preparation and stratification shape students' postsecondary entry into higher education and the labor market. Not only does the high school civics curriculum provide exposure to the political fabric of American democracy, but the coursework promotes political engagement, we argue, both directly through knowledge-building about the political system, identity development, and development of a sense of civic responsibility and indirectly through the effect of high school on educational attainment and labor market success. Integration into the social fabric of societal institutions beyond the family and the community often first occurs through school experiences. School activities like volunteering and extracurricular participation build social relationships and a sense of connection to the school. In combination, these three forms of integration—academic, civic, and social—encourage youth to vote in early adulthood.

Although we expect that many aspects of the high school experience, from course-taking and grades to volunteering and extracurricular involvement, would shape the political participation of children of both native-born and foreign-born parents, we hypothesize that children in immigrant families are positioned to benefit even more from these aspects of high school, for at least three reasons. First, children of immigrants typically achieve relatively high levels of academic success and engagement compared to native-born students of similar social, economic, and racial-ethnic backgrounds. This relative academic advantage may increase the saliency of what they learn in school, both social and academic. Second, because children of immigrants are less likely to have parents who are familiar with or engaged in the U.S. political system, their school experiences have a potentially greater impact on their political engagement. Third, children of immigrants, as inhabitants of two cultures, have experience in bridging two worlds and understanding multiple perspectives; this experience resonates with the central tenets of the high school social science curriculum and foreshadows an awareness of political issues and responsibility.

As we observe in chapter 1, the growth of the population of school-age children of immigrants, coupled with the low levels of youth political participation, underscores the need to better understand how schools prepare children of immigrants for their citizenship responsibilities. This book approaches this challenge by investigating our hypotheses, taking a multipronged approach: we conduct rigorous analysis of quantitative data with two recent large samples of adolescents in high schools who were followed as they transitioned into adulthood, and we use qualitative interviews with teachers and students to flesh out our understanding of the possible mechanisms through which schools shape the political behavior of children of immigrants. Before providing an overview of the organization of the book, we briefly describe our data.

Introduction to the Data

The quantitative component of our study utilized data from two nationally representative longitudinal surveys of students in high school: the Education Longitudinal Study of 2002 (ELS2002–2006) and the Adolescent Health and Academic Achievement Study (AHAA) and its partner study, the National Longitudinal Study of Adolescent Health (Add Health). Each of these databases contains school-based samples of adolescents and tracks them into early adulthood. Each database has strengths and weaknesses when it comes to addressing our research questions; taken together, they provide a more comprehensive and nuanced portrait of how adolescents' high school experiences shape their political participation in early adulthood. These data sets contain rich information on students' academic and social experiences in high school and on the high schools they attend. In particular, they provide detailed information about variables relevant to our research questions, such as student and parental nativity, students' social science preparation, and students' political participation (voting, voter registration, and identification with a political party), allowing us to analyze in depth the relationship between formal and informal schooling processes in adolescence and political participation in young adulthood among children of immigrants.

Information about the nativity of the parents and the student respondents is central to our research agenda and therefore deserves mention here. Although each of the two large and nationally representative databases has both strengths and limitations, we relied on the Add Health/AHAA more heavily for several reasons. Only Add Health asks respondents their citizenship status in early adulthood. Furthermore, although both data sets include reports from parents about their nativity, Add Health has more complete data because many parents did not respond to the ELS questionnaire and so the missing parents in that survey were disproportionately likely to be immigrant parents. On the other hand, ELS offers much richer data on students' academic achievement, both prior to entry into high school and along other dimensions. Notably, ELS administered reading and mathematics achievement tests, which are important components of achievement and provide important controls for understanding high school outcomes. Taken together, analyses of both databases, especially when the findings are consistent and suggest similar conclusions, assure us of the robustness of our findings. When possible, we have conducted parallel sensitivity analyses with both data sets and present findings that are robust, though we rarely show these supplemental analyses.

As mentioned earlier, we grouped together children of immigrants born in the United States and those born abroad. Because our central goal is to understand voting behavior, some analyses include only children of immigrants who are citizens, thus excluding first-generation immigrants who are not yet eligible to vote. Although we used only Add Health/AHAA, we did test similar models using ELS (where we probably included respondents who were ineligible to vote) and found similar results. More generally, our data analysis included testing for differences between first- and second-generation children of immigrants. Although there are some well-documented differences between these groups, particularly in their relationships with their parents and in some indicators of academic achievement (Harker 2001; Kalogrides 2009), we present these two groups of children of immigrants together for continuity, mentioning only notable differences between first- and second-generation students. Finally, we tested whether our conclusions about voting behavior varied by generational status—they did not. This result is not surprising because the group of first-generation citizens is already a select group.

In addition, we supplemented our quantitative analyses with interview-based data—collected through our New Citizens in a New Century research project—which offer a qualitative exploration of the perceptions of teachers and children of immigrants of the high school social science classroom and curriculum. This qualitative component of our study drew on interviews from two distinct groups of participants: nationally board-certified high school social science teachers and Latino, immigrant young adults in five key immigrant-receiving communities: New York, San Diego, Texas, Florida, and Chicago. While each region provided an ample population of Latino children of immigrants in the schools, each also offered a unique contextual perspective: that of the Cuban refugee in Florida, the historically Polish in Chicago, the Mexican in California and Texas, and the Dominican and Central American in New York. Although not central to the focus of our inquiry, these different student and teacher perspectives, as the careful reader will note, reflect the diversity of immigrant experiences and perspectives across these target communities.

Our target population of peer-recognized, board-certified teachers in these high-Latino, high-immigrant communities taught college preparatory social science courses, and the young adults took their social science courses with many of these same teachers. By carefully selecting our sample, engaging in data analysis during data collection, and using these processes to inform and shape further data collection (Charmaz 2006), we hope to shed light on the interactions between teachers and students in college preparatory social science courses, as perceived by both the teachers and the Latino young adults themselves.

These interviews were designed to complement our quantitative analysis by exploring—from both the teacher and student perspective—how the experiences of children of immigrants in the high school social science classroom shape their future political participation. For those readers interested in the sources and analytic methods utilized in this book, we describe our data, analytic samples, and research methodology in the appendix.

Overview of the Book

In chapter 1, we describe the demographic backdrop and political motivation for our study. We begin by presenting an overview of immigrants and immigration in the past decade, with a focus on the growing population of children of immigrants and the schools they attend. Then we explore trends in youth political participation across the past twenty years to explain our interest in outcomes focused on political participation.

Chapter 2 provides the theoretical foundation for our focus on schools as an important force in the political socialization and education of children of immigrants. We argue that the high school in particular is a valuable venue for inquiry because it serves adolescents as they are developing their independent identities and preparing for their transition to adulthood. In contrast to most research on children of immigrants, this study focuses on what schools do. Chapter 2 describes the rationale for this perspective.

In chapter 3, we explore immigrant adolescents' social positions with respect to their peers, family, and teachers, with a focus on the high school experience. Specifically, we describe how adolescent children of immigrants compare with their third-plus-generation peers on several dimensions of social integration and connection to their school that contribute to youths' sense of belonging in school: language preferences, extracurricular involvement, and social relationships. Our discussion of these connections sets the foundation for our exploration in chapter 4 of academic preparation and achievement among children of immigrants through an examination of their course-taking patterns and course grades. We explore these patterns not only by immigrant status but also by race and ethnicity, in order to address the racial and social stratification replicated in our school systems. Together, these two chapters provide insight into how adolescent children of immigrants are integrated into the institution of school and thus help us understand how formal and informal aspects of schooling influence their political participation in young adulthood.

In chapter 5, we narrow our focus to examine variation in social science preparation by generational status. As we have noted, social science coursework, because of its subject matter and promotion of civic values, is the formal component of schooling that we consider most relevant to adolescents' political development, and especially the political development of immigrant adolescents. Chapter 5 introduces this argument by investigating whether children of immigrants and children of native-born parents have similar social science experiences in high school. To answer this question, we analyzed differences by generational status in social science grades and in the number of social science credits taken in high school, while taking individual and school-level characteristics into account. Although we observed no differences in social science achievement, we found that children of immigrants take fewer social science courses in high school than do children of native-born parents. However, these differences are largely explained by differences in background characteristics, such as parental education.

In chapter 6, we investigate the relationship between formal and informal schooling processes in adolescence and political participation in young adulthood. We first examine whether the children of immigrants were more or less likely than children of native-born parents to register to vote and then to vote in the 2000 presidential election; we also analyze the likelihood that they would identify with any political party. Following these analyses, we investigate whether the associations between individual and school variables and political participation differ between children of immigrants and children of native-born parents.

Although children of immigrants and children of native-born parents look no different in terms of the likelihood of their registering and voting, we discovered that the factors associated with this likelihood are indeed very different; that is, the factors associated with the political participation of children of native-born parents are not necessarily the same as those that predict the political participation of children of immigrants. For children of native-born parents, background characteristics, such as parental education, as well as informal aspects of schooling, such as volunteering, are highly associated with political participation. For children of immigrants, however, parental education demonstrates no such predictive power for the likelihood of their registering and voting. Instead, social science coursework is the aspect of schooling most highly associated with the future political participation of children of immigrants in young adulthood. Similarly, we found that social science course-taking predicts whether students identify with a political party in early adulthood (although their coursework has nothing to do with *which* party they identify with). In contrast to the factors associated with registering and voting, however, course-taking predicts affiliation with a party for children of immigrants and native-born parents alike.

In chapter 7, we summarize our results and conclude with a discussion of the policy implications of our findings. High schools clearly play a role in shaping the civic development of young adults, and importantly, they appear to matter more in the civic development of children of immigrants. High school social science coursework in particular is central to the political participation of children of immigrants. Considering that children of immigrants make up an increasingly large segment of our nation's electorate, understanding the factors that shape their political participation is critical to our nation's civic vitality. Our findings point to one way in which schools might improve voter turnout among this growing population—by expanding access to social science curriculum in general and to advanced social science courses in particular.

CHAPTER 1

Immigration, U.S. Schools, and the Changing Youth Vote

with Molly Dondero

Recent, dramatic demographic changes in the school-age population initially prompted our questions about the political development of children of
immigrants. High rates of immigration to the United States over the last twenty
to thirty years, coupled with an unprecedented geographic dispersion of immigrants, have made immigrants and their children a growing presence throughout the country. As such, today's children of immigrants will have a major impact on the American educational and political systems for decades to come.

Although considerable research has examined the educational incorporation of children of immigrants, much less attention has been paid to understanding their political incorporation into U.S. civil society. Throughout this
book, we explore how the educational and political incorporation of children
of immigrants may be intertwined, hypothesizing that immigrant youths' experiences in the U.S. educational system during adolescence affect their political experiences later in young adulthood. As a first step in illustrating how
schools shape the political development of children of immigrants, we devote
the first part of this chapter to an overview of the characteristics of school-age
children of immigrants and the schools they attend.

A second, equally important component of our story is youth political
participation in the United States in general, which we must take into account in order to understand the political development of children of immigrants in young adulthood. Despite increases in the 2004 and 2008 presidential elections, youth voter turnout continues to be considerably lower than
that of the older adult population. Although social scientists recognize that
youth may be politically active in other, newer ways made possible by the expansion of technology and social media, young adult voting remains a source
of concern. Furthermore, there are important variations among young voters—by race-ethnicity and education, for example—that may also influence
the political assimilation of children of immigrants in young adulthood.

Focusing on these demographic and political developments, we first present an overview of recent U.S. immigration patterns, followed by profiles of the population of school-age children of immigrants and the high schools they attend. We end with a description of youth political participation in recent presidential elections. Taken together, these factors provide the backdrop for understanding the social context in which adolescent children of immigrants come of age politically in the United States.

Immigration to the United States Since the 1990s

Over the past two decades, the United States has experienced a tremendous increase in its foreign-born population. Numbering an estimated 37 million, foreign-born residents are now nearly 13 percent of the country's total population and account for more than 34 percent of the country's population growth since 2000 (Pew Hispanic Center 2009). Although immigration has decreased since 2005, it is nevertheless approaching peak rates from the late nineteenth and early twentieth centuries, when foreign-born residents made up 14.8 percent of the nation's population (Passel 2011). Demographers estimate that the United States will surpass this peak by 2050, when immigrants are projected to account for approximately 19 percent of the total population (Passel and Cohn 2008). The presence of children of immigrants in U.S. schools is likely to continue to grow in size and in diversity—social, ethnic, racial, and linguistic—in the coming decades.

The increase in the immigrant population has occurred alongside an unprecedented geographic diversification of immigrants in the United States (Fry 2006). For the past several decades, immigrants have been highly concentrated in six traditional settlement states: California, New York, Texas, Florida, New Jersey, and Illinois, especially Chicago (Massey and Capoferro 2008). Although these areas remain home to the majority of the country's foreign-born population, their overall share of immigrants has decreased since the 1990s. In contrast, between 1990 and 2000, the proportion of immigrants in twenty-two "new growth" states in middle America has increased dramatically (Urban Institute 2002). In particular, South Carolina, Arkansas, Nevada, Tennessee, and Alabama have experienced the greatest growth in foreign-born population since 2000 (Pew Hispanic Center 2009). The type of communities in which immigrants settle is also changing. Whereas immigrants traditionally were concentrated in urban centers (Zhou 2009), recent settlement patterns point to increased movement of immigrants into rural areas, small towns, and suburbs around the country (Massey and Capoferro 2008). With this growth and geographic dispersal of the foreign-born population, more immigrants than ever before are present in more communities throughout the country. Consequently, many more of our nation's institutions, such as schools, labor markets, and the political system, now serve immigrants and face the task of facilitating their incorporation into the country's social structure.

In addition to growth and geographic spread, today's foreign-born population is also characterized by its youth and its relatively high fertility rates compared to the native-born population. More than half of the country's recently arrived immigrants are of childbearing age (Passel 2011). In 2008 the fertility rate among the foreign-born was 2.7 children per woman, compared with 2.0 children for native-born women; in addition, births to foreign-born women accounted for nearly 25 percent of all U.S. births (Passel and Taylor 2010). The growth of the immigrant population, together with continued immigration to the United States, signals that the population of children of immigrants will be growing for decades to come. These demographic shifts have major implications for the U.S. educational and political systems. In the next section, we provide a descriptive portrait of school-age children of immigrants to show how immigration is changing the face of the nation's schools and future electorate.

Profile of School-Age Children of Immigrants

Children of immigrants, particularly those of Latin American origin, represent the fastest-growing sector of the U.S. youth population (Capps et al. 2005; Stepick and Dutton-Stepick 2002). Through the year 2050, children of immigrants are projected to account for nearly all of the growth among the population of children age seventeen and younger in the United States, with their share of the total U.S. youth population increasing from nearly one-fourth in 2008 to one-third in 2050 (Capps et al. 2005; Fix and Passel 2003; Passel 2011; Passel and Cohn 2008). The rapid growth of this population will compel U.S. schools and educators to serve children of immigrants in larger numbers than ever before and especially to adjust their services to meet the unique linguistic, academic, and social needs of this group of students.

Although the United States has long been home to a large population of children of immigrants—especially following the waves of mass immigration in the late nineteenth and early twentieth centuries—today's children of immigrants differ markedly from their earlier counterparts. In nearly all respects, from national origin to race and ethnicity to home language to place of residence, today's children of immigrants are a more diverse group than their predecessors (Tienda and Haskins 2011; Zhou 1997a). Whereas most children of immigrants from earlier waves of immigration were white and of European descent, today's children of immigrants are largely nonwhite and come primarily from Latin America and Asia (Hernandez 2004), with Mexico, the Dominican Republic, Haiti, India, Korea, China, and the Philippines representing the most common countries of origin (Capps et al. 2005). The racial and ethnic diversity of contemporary children of immigrants has contributed to an increasingly complex process of incorporation, which is already complicated by the pressure on many immigrants and their children to confront a highly racialized U.S. society.

Although the diversity of national origins makes for an equally rich tapestry of home languages, it has raised concern about the English proficiency of children of immigrants. Considerable current research points, however, to the rapid acquisition of English among the children of immigrants in the United States (Olsen 2000; Portes 2002; Portes and Hao 1998), often at the expense of their primary language. If the conventional wisdom is that prior generations of immigrants acquired English more quickly than immigrants today, and with greater facility, empirical evidence soundly refutes any such claim (Wilkerson and Salmons 2008). In fact, in many ways immigrant parents of past generations were better able than contemporary immigrants to maintain the native language, both in the home and in the schools, while their children added English to their repertoire. German-language schools, for instance, enjoyed a rich civic and cultural role in the development of the American education system over its first century and a half (Kloss 1977; Wiley 2007). Between World Wars I and II, however, the discourse of Americanization shifted to emphasize linguistic assimilation among the foreign-born population (Pavlenko 2002), mirroring the isolationist tendencies of that era, and some of the highly publicized concerns about the English proficiency of the foreign-born population today continue to reflect a fear of immigrants bordering on xenophobia (see, for example, Huntington 2004). More often, however, with the American identity so heavily intertwined with proficiency in English (Mertz 1982), nationalism is often expressed through a concern that immigrants are not learning English quickly enough. In fact, the rise of the current English-only movement (Schildkraut 2003; Wiley and Wright 2004) is not surprising given that the rate at which children of immigrants learn English and ostensibly "become American" is one of the most easily measured markers of the adoption of the American identity.

Although the transition to English dominance now occurs within one generation (Portes and Hao 1998), roughly 18 percent of school-age children of immigrants report speaking a language other than English in the home and not speaking English very well (Fortuny 2010). The U.S. Department of Education's Office of English Language Acquisition (OELA) reports that among the 5 million language minority students identified by the schools as limited English proficient (LEP) or as an English learner (EL), more than four hundred different languages are spoken. The most common languages among the EL student population are Spanish (79.6 percent), Vietnamese (2.4 percent), and Hmong (1.8 percent) (Hopstock and Stephenson 2003). Furthermore, more than 60 percent of all children of immigrants have one or two parents with limited English proficiency, and a full 23 percent of school-age children of immigrants live in linguistically isolated households in which no one over the age of fourteen speaks English very well (Capps et al. 2004; Fortuny 2010). Despite these potential linguistic obstacles, in U.S. schools children of immigrants are generally expected both to learn English and to learn *in* English.

In addition to their linguistic diversity, today's children of immigrants also demonstrate remarkable diversity with respect to where they live in the United States. Figure 1.1 shows the dramatic growth and geographic dispersal of the population of school-age children of immigrants between 1990 and 2008. Although the majority of children of immigrants remain concentrated in the six traditional settlement areas, the recent geographic diversification of the foreign-born population has made children of immigrants a growing presence in all states, and subsequently in schools across the country as well. In particular, North Carolina, Nebraska, Arkansas, Nevada, Georgia, and Iowa have experienced the greatest increases in their population of children of immigrants.

The growth in immigrants' numbers and geographic diversification suggests that schools and educators all over the United States now provide a primary source of education for children of immigrants. Today schools and regions that historically have had very few immigrant residents must address the educational needs of a growing population of children of immigrants (Wortham, Murillo, and Hamann 2002). Indeed, our calculations from school district data in the 1990 U.S. census and the 2008 American Community Survey (ACS) attest to this fact. We found that the proportion of school districts enrolling at least twenty-five children of immigrants more than doubled from 1990 (46 percent) to 2008 (96 percent). These numbers show that nearly all of the country's school districts now serve at least some children of immigrants.

Many children of immigrants experience risk factors that may threaten their educational success (Hernandez 2004), such as poverty, low levels of parental education, and uncertain legal status. Roughly half of all children of immigrants live in low-income households, compared with 35 percent of children of native-born parents, and 21 percent of children of immigrants live below the poverty line, compared with 15 percent of children of native-born parents (Fortuny 2010). On average, immigrant parents also have markedly lower levels of education than native-born parents: more than one-quarter of children of immigrants have parents with less than a high school education, compared with only 7 percent of children of native-born parents, though the disparities are smaller at the higher end of the educational spectrum (Chaudry and Fortuny 2010). Citizenship issues further complicate the lives of many children of immigrants. Nearly three-quarters of the more than 17 million children of immigrants under age eighteen are native-born and thus are U.S. citizens by birth, but approximately 5 million of them live with undocumented parents (Capps et al. 2005; Fix and Passel 2003; Urban Insti-

Figure 1.1.   Share of Children of Immigrants Ages Five to Seventeen, by State, 1990 and 2008

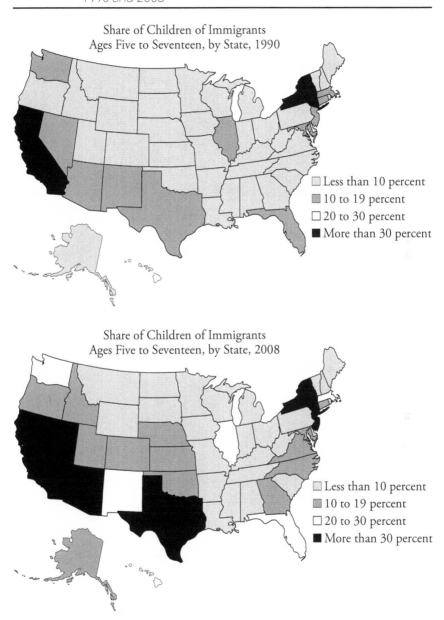

Share of Children of Immigrants
Ages Five to Seventeen, by State, 1990

☐ Less than 10 percent
▨ 10 to 19 percent
☐ 20 to 30 percent
■ More than 30 percent

Share of Children of Immigrants
Ages Five to Seventeen, by State, 2008

☐ Less than 10 percent
▨ 10 to 19 percent
☐ 20 to 30 percent
■ More than 30 percent

Source: Authors' calculation of data from the 1990 U.S. Census and American Community Survey, (2006–2008), National Center for Education Statistics, School and Demographic System.

tute 2006). Children living in undocumented or mixed-status households often lack access to public services, and their parents may limit interaction with schools and other institutions for fear of deportation.

The racial, ethnic, cultural, and social differences between today's children of immigrants and the children of earlier European immigrants, as well as the differences between today's children of immigrants and children of native-born parents, have given rise to an academic debate about the long-term mobility prospects of contemporary children of immigrants. Some scholars have argued that these children will follow a path that is similar to, albeit slower than, the path of the children of earlier European immigrants, who largely assimilated into the American middle-class mainstream (Alba and Nee 1997). Others contend that because of their different individual characteristics and contextual circumstances, today's children of immigrants will not experience a uniform ascent into the middle-class mainstream but rather will undergo a "segmented assimilation" into various strata of American society, with many at risk of downward mobility (Portes and Zhou 1993). Although our analyses do not directly address this debate, we frame our study around one of the central tenets of segmented assimilation theory—that contextual influences interact with individual characteristics to shape the incorporation of children of immigrants (Portes and Zhou 1993). Specifically, we argue that children of immigrants' individual characteristics interact with the contextual influences of their schools to shape their political incorporation in young adulthood. As described here, those individual characteristics suggest that schools are likely to face significant challenges in meeting the needs of the country's changing school-age population and in helping children of immigrants to overcome these barriers. The future of these children and ultimately the nation depends on the ability of schools to prepare them not only for postsecondary education and labor market participation but also for civic life.

Profile of the High Schools Serving Children of Immigrants

For children of immigrants, schools are a critical context of reception. Not only do schools represent a primary site of social and bureaucratic incorporation, but they also provide the knowledge and skills necessary for postsecondary education and employment. Social scientists have identified several school-level characteristics associated with the assimilation of children of immigrants. For example, Alejandro Portes and Min Zhou (1993) highlight the role of a school's socioeconomic status (SES) and its concentration of minority students. They argue that many of the children of immigrants concentrated in low-income urban areas attend resource-poor schools where they come into contact with the anti-education "oppositional culture" of some native-born minority youth. Exposure to poor-quality education and adversarial attitudes toward education may threaten the academic success of children of immigrants and increase their risk of downward mobility. Other school attributes besides school SES and minority concentration—both structural and relational in nature—influence the educational outcomes of children of immigrants (Hao and Pong 2008). Structural attributes are characteristics such as school sector, demographic composition, and course and program offerings. Relational attributes are based in the interpersonal facets of schooling and include academic climate, teacher-student relations, and teachers' and administrators' sense of collective responsibility for students.

In the following section, we provide an idea of the educational contexts of children of immigrants by using some of our previously published research (Dondero and Muller, forthcoming) to show what such attributes look like in public high schools serving Latino students. We focus on schools serving Latino students rather than schools serving children of immigrants because most school- and district-level data sets do not collect information about the nativity of students' parents. We recognize that this is not a perfect approach because not all Latino children are children of immigrants; many have native-born parents and U.S. roots that go back many generations. However, given that Latinos make up the largest and fastest-growing segment of the children of immigrants population, we believe that this is the best available proxy. It is important to note that only the analyses presented in table 1.1 rely on the school- and district-level data sets lacking measures of student and parent nativity. All subsequent analyses use nationally collected survey data from random samples of adolescents, and these data sets do include such measures.

We describe high schools in terms of their demographic characteristics, instructional resources, and quality of education. We also disaggregate schools according to both the concentration of Latino students enrolled in the district and the growth in the district's Latino student population between 1990 and 2000. We refer to schools in areas with a high (above-average) concentration of Latino students as "established Latino destination districts," and schools with a relatively low concentration of Latino students but exceptionally high rates of growth between 1990 and 2000 as "new Latino destination districts." Looking at schools in these different settings provides a sense of the diversity of educational contexts encountered by Latino high school students.

We first describe the demographic characteristics of schools. Table 1.1 shows that schools in new and established Latino destinations looked quite different in terms of their location, racial and ethnic composition, and SES. Schools in new destinations were located primarily in rural areas or small towns, whereas schools in established destinations were located mainly in urban settings. In addition, schools in new destinations enrolled significantly lower average percentages of minority students, LEP students, and students eligible for free or reduced-cost lunch.

Table 1.1   Public High Schools by Latino Destination District Type, 2000

Latino Destination District Type	New (710 Schools)		Established (1,200 Schools)		Significant Difference
Demographic and compositional attributes (2,300 schools)					
Urbanicity					
Urban	0.10		0.33		*
Suburban	0.45		0.44		
Small town/rural	0.45		0.24		*
Mean percentage of minority students enrolled	19.73%	(23.16)	44.53%	(31.78)	*
Mean percentage of LEP students enrolled	1.39%	(5.98)	5.50%	(10.78)	*
Mean percentage of students eligible for free lunch	26.75%	(23.59)	40.9%	(30.18)	*
Quality of education indicators					
Graduation and college-going rates (2,270 schools with twelfth-grade students enrolled)					
Twelfth-graders who graduated this year	90.94%	(18.23)	85.65%	(24.00)	*
Graduates who enrolled in four-year college	40.38%	(22.59)	33.77%	(25.33)	*
Graduates who enrolled in two-year college	20.48%	(15.21)	24.16%	(18.03)	*
Graduates who enrolled in tech school	8.70%	(8.88)	8.74%	(11.55)	
Linguistic support services					
Methods used to identify LEP students (1,480 schools with any LEP students enrolled)					
Information provided by parent	0.91		0.92		
Teacher observation or referral	0.88		0.86		
Home language survey	0.63		0.81		*
Student interview	0.90		0.87		
Student records	0.93		0.95		
Achievement tests	0.51		0.61		*

Table 1.1   (Continued)

Latino Destination District Type	New (710 Schools)		Established (1,200 schools)		Significant Difference
Language proficiency tests	0.67		0.84		*
Number of methods used	5.44	(1.47)	5.85	(1.40)	*
Specific LEP instruction offered	0.84		0.92		*
Type of LEP instruction offered (1,310 schools offering specific LEP instruction)					
ESL, bilingual, or structured immersion	0.94		0.95		
Native-language maintenance instruction	0.28		0.40		*
Instruction in regular English classroom	0.89		0.91		
Language of subject matter courses for LEP students					
Native language	0.08		0.18		*
English	0.93		0.91		
Both languages	0.74		0.80		*
Additional methods of LEP instruction					
Remedial/compensatory classes	0.60		0.61		
Special education	0.28		0.38		*
Regular classes	0.94		0.97		

Source: National Center for Education Statistics, Schools and Staffing Survey, 1999 to 2000.
Notes: Means or proportions shown, with standard deviations in parentheses for continuous variables. Data are weighted. Per NCES restricted-use data guidelines, unweighted frequencies are rounded to the nearest 10.
*Significantly different at $p < .05$.

The more affluent socioeconomic profiles of the new destination schools suggest that they offered better resources and educational opportunities, and we see some evidence of this in the quality-of-education indicators. For example, schools in new destinations significantly outranked schools in established destinations on high school graduation and four-year college enrollment rates. In new destination schools, an average of 91 percent of seniors graduated from high school and an average of 40 percent of graduating seniors enrolled in a four-year college, compared to only 86 percent and 34 percent, respectively, in established destination schools.

In addition, we found differences in some of the instructional resources available to Latino high school students in the new and established destinations—in particular, the linguistic support services. For example, schools in new destinations relied most heavily on anecdotal methods of identifying LEP students, such as teacher observations, parent information, student interviews, and student records. Although schools in established destinations also relied on these methods, they were significantly more likely than schools in new destinations to also consult systematic diagnostic evaluations such as language proficiency tests, achievement tests, and home language surveys. This suggests that schools in established destinations had a wider range of diagnostic instruments available and might have been better equipped to identify students' linguistic needs.

The linguistic support services offered also varied in prevalence and type. Of schools that reported enrolling LEP- or EL-identified students, 92 percent in established destinations offered specific linguistic support services to these students, compared to only 84 percent in new destinations. Of schools that offered specific LEP services, schools in new and established destinations were equally likely to offer ESL, bilingual, or structured immersion instruction, to offer instruction in the regular English classroom, and to teach subject matter courses to LEP students in English. However, significantly more schools in established destinations offered native-language maintenance instruction to LEP and EL students and taught subject matter courses in the students' native language.

This descriptive portrait of schools suggests that the educational circumstances of Latino high school students are both varied and complex. Whereas in the past the concentration of Latinos in a handful of cities within a handful of states may have made for more homogenous educational experiences, the recent growth and dispersion of the Latino population has opened up a great variety of educational contexts for the children of this population. We argue that the wide variety of educational contexts experienced by Latinos today warrants increased research attention focused on school contextual factors in analyses of adolescent immigrant incorporation. The need to address school factors is thus especially critical in analyses of understudied aspects of incorporation, such as political incorporation.

Profile of Youth Political Participation Since the 1990s

The growth of the population of children of immigrants has implications not only for the country's educational system but also for its political system. Indeed, their integration into the political system over the next few decades will largely determine the country's future civic health (Stepick and Dutton-Stepick 2002). With their growing numbers and diverse backgrounds, immigrants have the power to infuse new ideas into politics and define important political issues (Plotke 1999). It will take time for the children of immigrants to achieve their full political potential in the United States, but politicians and lawmakers already recognize their growing electoral importance (Durand, Telles, and Flashman 2006; Suro 2005). In this vein, many studies have explored the political participation of immigrant adults in the United States (DeSipio 2001; Ramakrishnan 2005; Ramakrishnan and Espenshade 2001), but relatively little research has examined the political participation of immigrant youth (Stepick and Dutton-Stepick 2002). The impending impact of children of immigrants on the nation's political system underscores the need for such studies. Their political behavior is inevitably influenced by their parents, but research is needed on the ways in which their paths to political participation diverge from those of their parents.

To understand the political development of children of immigrants, it is necessary to first understand overall youth political participation in the United States. In discussions of civic engagement in this country, youth political participation—or rather, the lack thereof—remains a persistent source of concern (Levine 2007; Shea and Green 2007). Indeed, the levels of political involvement among today's eighteen- to twenty-four-year-olds are notoriously low. Although today's youth generation outpaces older generations on some measures of civic engagement, such as volunteering and community involvement, they fall far behind their elders on measures of political participation, especially voter turnout and membership in political organizations (Shea and Green 2007; Zukin et al. 2006). To better understand the political behavior of today's youth, we briefly review trends in voter registration, voter turnout, and partisan preference among eighteen- to twenty-four-year-old citizens during the 1996 to 2008 presidential elections. We chose to begin with the 1996 election because this was the first election that the adolescents in our data sets would have been old enough to remember. (The youngest would have been about ten years old at the time).

Voter registration rates among young adults have inched up steadily in the last four presidential election cycles. As shown in figure 1.2, 58.5 percent of eligible young adults reported having registered to vote in time for the 2008 presidential election, compared with only 48 percent in 1996. Despite this promising increase, voter registration rates among young adults remain much lower than those of older adults, whose reported registration rates ranged from 68 to 75 percent across the 1996 to 2008 election years.

As we might expect, age disparities in voter turnout are similar to those in voter registration. As shown in figure 1.3, younger voters have turned out in much lower numbers than older voters in every presidential election since 1996. However, the age gap began to narrow in 2004, owing to a remarkable jump in the youth voter turnout: between the 2000 and 2004 presidential elections, youth voter turnout increased by an impressive eleven percentage points, from 36 percent to 47 percent. An additional increase of two percent-

Figure 1.2.   Citizen Voter Registration by Age, U.S. Presidential Elections,
              1996 to 2008

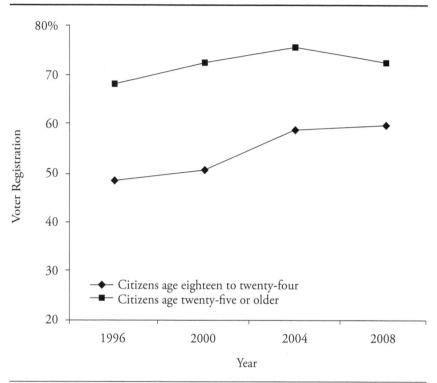

Source: Authors' tabulation of data from U.S. Census Bureau and Department of Labor, Current Population Survey 1996–2008, November Voting and Registration Supplements.

age points continued this upward trend in 2008, though in much less dramatic fashion. It is important to point out, however, that this upward trend may not necessarily signal a long-term improvement in youth voter turnout. It may instead be the result of particular period effects, such as President Barack Obama's mobilization of the youth vote in 2008, increased concern about issues such as the wars in Iraq and Afghanistan, or the financial crises. Data from midterm elections, which reveal no such increase in voter turnout among eighteen- to twenty-four-year-olds, suggest that this may indeed have been the case. In fact, there was a very slight decrease in voter turnout for this age group between the 2006 and 2010 midterm elections. Overall, young adult voter turnout in midterm elections since 1998 has averaged about 21 percent, less than half of the voter turnout rate among the twenty-five and older population (Center for Information and Research on Civic Learning

Figure 1.3.   Citizen Voter Turnout by Age, U.S. Presidential Elections, 1996 to 2008

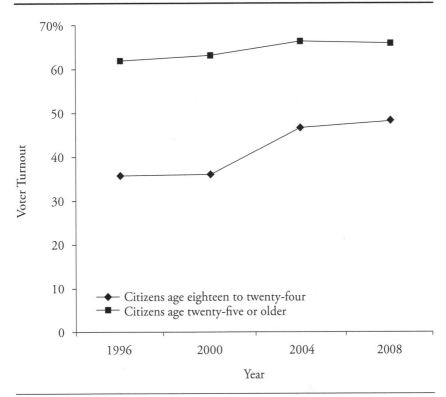

Source: Authors' tabulation of data from U.S. Census Bureau and Department of Labor, Current Population Survey 1996–2008, November Voting and Registration Supplements.

and Engagement 2011). Despite recent increases in youth voter turnout, the overall rate remains markedly lower than that of the older adult population.

Turning to comparisons within the young adult population, we see that voting rates vary considerably by sociodemographic characteristics such as gender, education, race, and parental nativity. For example, during the last four presidential elections, young women consistently voted at higher rates than young men. In fact, in 2008 the gender gap among young voters was the widest in recent history, with 52 percent of female eighteen- to twenty-four-year-olds voting, compared with only 45 percent of their male counterparts (Kirby and Kawashima-Ginsberg 2009). Young people with some college experience also voted in much higher numbers than their peers with no college experience. Figure 1.4 shows youth voter turnout by educational at-

Figure 1.4.   Eighteen- to Twenty-Four-Year-Old Citizen Voter Turnout by Education, U.S. Presidential Elections, 1996 to 2008

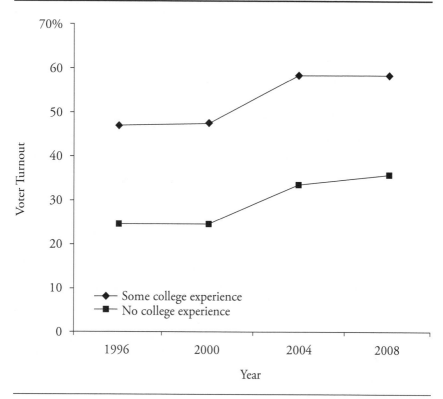

Source: Authors' tabulation of data from U.S. Census Bureau and Department of Labor, Current Population Survey 1996–2008, November Voting and Registration Supplements.

tainment (some college experience versus no college experience). In each of the past four presidential elections, young adults with a college degree or some college experience voted at rates that were more than twenty percentage points higher than those of their peers with no college experience.

Until the 2008 presidential election, racial disparities among young voters were also fairly consistent across years. Figure 1.5 reveals racial-ethnic differences in youth voter turnout rates. Young white adults voted at slightly higher rates than young black adults and at considerably higher rates than Asian and Latino young adults in the 1996 to 2004 presidential elections. In 2008, however, young black voters reversed this trend, turning out to the polls in record numbers and surpassing the voter turnout rates of young adults from all other racial groups. Figure 1.6 shows that youth voter turnout further var-

Figure 1.5.   Eighteen- to Twenty-Four-Year-Old Citizen Voter Turnout by
Race-Ethnicity, U.S. Presidential Elections, 1996 to 2008

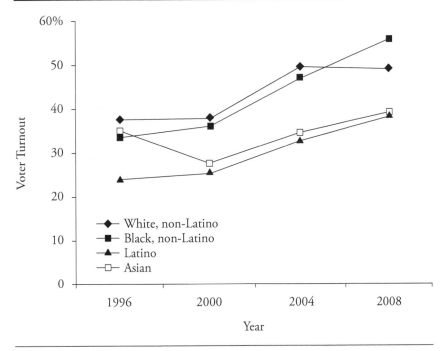

Source: Authors' tabulation of data from U.S. Census Bureau and Department of Labor, Current Population Survey 1996–2008, November Voting and Registration Supplements.

ied by parental nativity as well as race-ethnicity.[1] We do not observe a single pattern of voter turnout across the children of immigrants groups. Instead, we see that their participation in the 1996 to 2008 presidential elections varied in complicated ways that probably reflect both period effects and changes over time in the composition of the U.S. immigrant population.

Comparisons across immigrant-race groups indicate that since the 2000 presidential election, the two largest groups of children of immigrants in the United States—Latinos and Asians—have had considerably lower voter turnout rates than white and black children of native-born parents and white children of immigrants. Like children of native-born parents, however, Latino and Asian children of immigrants experienced an upward trend in their voter turnout rates after the 2000 presidential election, though the magnitude of the increase was much smaller for Latino children of immigrants relative to all other groups. Voter turnout among white children of immigrants, on the other hand, looks quite different from that of Latino and Asian chil-

Figure 1.6.   Eighteen- to Twenty-Four-Year-Old Citizen Voter Turnout by
              Parental Nativity and Race-Ethnicity, U.S. Presidential Elections,
              1996 to 2008

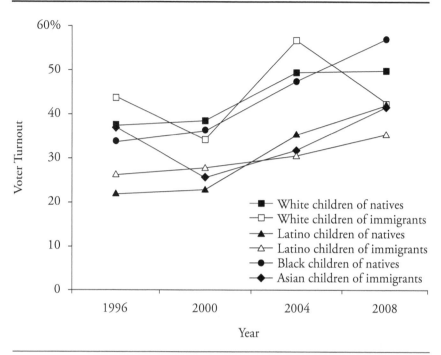

Source: Authors' tabulation of data from U.S. Census Bureau and Department of Labor, Current Population Survey 1996–2008, November Voting and Registration Supplements.

dren of immigrants in that, with the exception of the 2008 presidential election, their voter turnout rates have been similar to or higher than those of white and black children of native-born parents.

In addition, the trend in voter turnout among white children of immigrants diverges from the trends for all other immigrant-race groups in that it has been characterized by sharp decreases and increases in alternating presidential election years. However, we interpret the numbers for this group with caution because white children of immigrants are an even more ethnically heterogeneous group than Asian and Latino children of immigrants. Turning to a within-race comparison, we see an interesting crossover in voter turnout rates among Latino children of immigrants and Latino children of native-born parents. Whereas in the 1996 and 2000 presidential elections Latino children of immigrants had higher voter turnout rates than did Latino children of U.S.-born parents, this gap was reversed in the 2004 and 2008 presidential elections. Again, the changes in the voter turnout rate among the Latino children of immigrants may reflect shifts in the composition of the population of Latino immigrant parents, just as it may reflect shifts in an era's partisan topics of debate.

Political party identification among young adults provides additional insight into their levels of political engagement. Political parties promote civic engagement by integrating citizens into the political process and helping to create civic-minded citizens (Gimpel, Lay, and Schuknecht 2003; Shea and Green 2007). Partisan preference among young registered voters has leaned increasingly toward the Democratic Party since 1996. In 1996, 50 percent of young registered voters identified as Democrat, while 44 percent identified as Republican. In 2008 the gap was much wider, with 58 percent of young registered voters identifying as Democrat, compared to only 33 percent identifying as Republican (Keeter, Horowitz, and Tyson 2008).

Collectively, the trends in political party identification, voter registration, and voter turnout that we have highlighted in this chapter create a complex portrait of contemporary youth political participation in the United States that can be characterized by substantial variation between the young adult and older adult populations, within the young adult population itself, and over time. Seeking to better understand such variation, social scientists have found that a variety of factors, both individual and contextual, shape young adults' patterns of political and civic involvement. In addition to sociodemographic characteristics such as gender, race-ethnicity, and education, other traits such as parental education, academic achievement, extracurricular involvement, and religiosity also predict political participation in early adulthood (Putnam 2000; Zukin et al. 2006). Young adults' attitudes toward and interest in politics, as well as their perceived ability to effect social change, may also influence their political participation. Studies have shown that, compared with past generations, today's youth are less interested in and less informed about politics, and less likely to view voting as a civic duty (Zukin et al. 2006). In addition, contemporary young adults report feeling the ability to effect change on the local level, but not necessarily the national level (Flanagan and Faison 2001; National Association of Secretaries of State 2000; Youniss et al. 2002). Together, these and other studies form a large body of research that has shown that young adults' political development, like other processes of adolescent development, is multifaceted and highly dependent on a number of diverse individual and contextual factors.

Despite the well-established body of literature on the political development of young adults in the United States, we know little about how this process unfolds for children of immigrants. Questions remain about the applicability of traditional explanatory models to the political and civic development of this population. Do traditional explanations of youth political participation hold for children of immigrants? Do the individual and contextual factors that shape the political behavior of third-plus-generation adolescents similarly shape the political behavior of first- and second-generation adolescents? Differences in the life experiences and the academic, linguistic, and social profiles of children of immigrants and children of native-born parents provide us with compelling reason to believe that political socialization for immigrant adolescents in U.S. high schools may also be different.

CHAPTER 2

Adolescents' Families, Schools, and Communities: Shaping Political Engagement in Young Adulthood

During adolescence in America, an individual's social world widens greatly. As a child, his or her world and identity development were centered in the family and the home. During adolescence, however, the individual begins to branch out, making connections with friends and other community members beyond the fold of the home. The world of the adolescent expands largely through the school—through relationships with peers, teachers, and mentors and the social networks that shape the educational experience. This is not to say that families and communities are no longer important, but rather that schools are uniquely situated to have a major impact on the development of adolescents—including their political development.

Adolescence is a pivotal period for developing a political identity and becoming politically engaged, and adolescent political development often affects early adult political behavior (Atkins and Hart 2003; Callahan, Muller, and Schiller 2008; Frisco, Muller, and Dodson 2004; Glanville 1999). In fact, adolescents and young adults have led the charge in several recent movements for political and social change, just as they have at other points in history (Jennings, Stoker, and Bowers 2009). The youth vote mobilized in response to Barack Obama's campaign in the 2008 election (Kirby and Kawashima-Ginsberg 2009), as well as around the Iraq War in 2004 (López, Kirby, and Sagoff 2005). And perhaps most central to our thesis, the potential political importance of the relatively young and growing immigrant population was highlighted in 2006 when the rallies on behalf of immigrant rights were led largely by the adolescent and young adult children of immigrant parents (Bloemraad and Trost 2008; Seif 2011). Issues related to immigrants and immigration remain at the forefront of the political debate; the children of immigrants coming of age today no doubt have a heightened awareness of what is at stake in elections compared to their peers with native-born parents.

In many ways, the social and educational experiences of children of immigrants during adolescence are likely to parallel those of their peers with native-born parents, but their experiences will also differ in substantive and significant ways. As children of immigrants come of age, they must navigate not only the culture and perspective of their parents but also those of the school and the outside world. With this in mind, we consider the range of experiences that shape political development, especially among children of immigrants.

Immigrant Adolescents, Their Families, and Their Political Socialization

The family-based transmission of political behaviors and ideologies has been well documented (Jennings et al. 2009; Miller and Shanks 1996), but research findings on such transmission may be more applicable to children of native-born parents than to children of immigrants, since patterns of political socialization among immigrant families have been less comprehensively studied. The existing research on immigrant families points to bidirectional patterns of political influence from children to parents as well as from parents to children (Bloemraad and Trost 2008; Wong and Tseng 2007). Although family and community are certainly central to the political development of all youth, we argue that in the immigrant family the experiences of adolescent children and the intergenerational changes associated with the immigrant family's adaptation make the socializing experiences of school particularly important in the political socialization of these children.

Many of the teachers in our qualitative inquiry referred to what they perceived to be a role reversal between children of immigrants and their parents in the sharing of political and civic understanding. The teachers were particularly aware of how these children connected their lives in school with their lives at home. Mr. Rocca, a European history teacher in Florida, aptly noted that his immigrant students often brought the content of the class to the dinner table.

> Even if it's not formally a part of the curriculum, the kids will go home and talk to their parents about it. . . . I know from my own personal experience that some of the things that we have talked about, the kids have gone home and talked to their parents, and the parents have become more civically active when the kids explain it to them, even if it is in Spanish, for example.

Having already negotiated a somewhat difficult political construct in class, children of immigrants in this class then take that concept home for further discussion—often, as Mr. Rocca indicated, in the parents' native language. Mr. Rocca was not the only high school social science teacher in our study who recognized the position of immigrant students as they not only navigated relatively new political concepts but also conveyed them to their parents, and several teachers also noted that such intergenerational shaping of political understanding was facilitated by the student's use of the home language.

As a marker of relationships, language is one of the most salient and symbolic ties to family and community for children of immigrants. Adolescents' decisions about their use of the home language may ultimately determine the breadth and depth of their relationships with family, community, and school (Bankston and Zhou 1995; Johnson, Stein, and Wrinkle 2003; Stanton-Salazar and Dornbusch 1995). Likewise, loss and atrophy of the home language may separate children of immigrants from potentially supportive coethnic ties within the family and the larger immigrant community (Rumbaut and Portes 2001; Vigil and Yun 1998). As children of immigrants transition from the K-12 school system into adult civic and professional society, maintenance of the home language may or may not diminish in importance, depending on the community context (Golash-Boza 2005). Strong social networks facilitate new immigrants' successful integration into U.S. society academically, economically, and politically (Portes and Rumbaut 2001; Sanders and Nee 1996), and both home-language and English proficiency can determine the shape and strength of these networks. Just as language may symbolize the connections between U.S. society, family, community, and country of origin, adolescent children of immigrants engage with their new country at a pivotal point in their own development marked by their family's adaptation to a new culture and their own growing independence from their parents.

Neighborhood and community composition influences the integration of immigrants into U.S. society, through both segregation (Schmid 2001) and access to social networks and their accompanying social capital (Bankston and Zhou 1997; Portes and Allepick 1993). The social capital available through coethnic communities in traditional receiving areas has been heavily documented, but much less is known about these school and community ties in new immigrant destinations (Waters and Jiménez 2005). Whether children of immigrants fare better or worse than the children of native-born parents, or about the same, remains to be explored.

Churches and religious organizations also shape the engagement of new immigrants in U.S. society. Religious institutions often provide network access through a shared belief system as well as organized community activities (Verba, Schlozman, and Brady 1995). The intersection of religious and linguistic identities is of special interest to any study of the development of an engaged, participatory citizenry. For example, the Catholic Church has begun to promote Latino immigrants' maintenance of their ethnic and linguistic identities to facilitate their integration into a new society (Levitt 2002). The church's recognition of the importance of the home language and the coethnic community resonates with the importance of community among immigrant youth. In U.S. society more generally, involvement in religious organizations is strongly associated with political participation, both directly (for example, through voter registration drives) (Kelley and De Graaf 1997) and indirectly through a sense of affiliation and ties to formal community-based organizations.

The Political Socialization of Immigrant Youth: Schools and Schooling

For children of immigrants, late adolescence and the transition to early adulthood may also be marked by the emergence of new relationships with family, community, and ethnic identity. The pathways for these relationships and community connections may be similar to those of their peers with native-born parents, though the significance of the relationships and how they contrast with family culture or ethnicity may be different. Some argue that children of immigrants, through segmented, marginalized opportunities at school or in the neighborhood, are more likely to come in contact with native-born minority youths who embrace an oppositional culture (Portes and Zhou 1993; Rodríguez 2003), but others argue that there is little evidence of this (Cortes 2006). Nevertheless, the relationships formed by children of immigrants, particularly in school, may provide important clues about the development of their political behavior during the transition to adulthood.

Three key aspects of the social expansion that is adolescence have been found to have an impact on political participation in young adulthood. First and foremost in most people's minds are the social aspects of school that arise through extracurricular involvement. As noted previously, volunteering and participating in extracurricular activities strengthen ties between students and their peers and teachers, while also helping to define their role as part of a community. We investigate these social aspects of school in the next chapter. Second, a primary mission of high schools is to prepare adolescents for the transition to young adulthood, in particular for entrance into college or the workforce. The stratifying aspects of the ways in which schools carry out this mission have been much discussed, especially with respect to how stratification reproduces inequalities across generations. Children of immigrants who live in poor communities and attend schools of lower quality may be especially vulnerable to this social aspect of schooling and its effects on their academic achievement. Because educational attainment is an important determinant of voting behavior in adulthood, we investigate this aspect of schools' potential role in the transition to adulthood. Third, and finally, schools play a central role in the political development of youth through a political and civic curriculum designed to provide them with experiences that will inform their political involvement into and during adulthood. We investigate the aspects of social science curriculum that might relate to political engagement in chapter 5. In chapter 6, we investigate the roles of each of these components of the adolescents' experiences in high school—social involvement, academic achievement, and exposure to social science curriculum—in their voting behavior in early adulthood. Here we turn to a review of the literature that motivates each of these dimensions of inquiry.

THE SOCIAL ASPECTS OF SCHOOL

Adolescence is a time to gain independence, form new relationships, take on new social roles, and begin to make choices about group membership and affiliations. Volunteering, peer relationships, and extracurricular involvement are all aspects of social integration during adolescence that may shape future political participation. Through high schools, children of immigrants gain exposure and access to a peer-based social structure through which they can become involved with organized social and extracurricular activities that allow them to engage with a community outside of their families. Integration into the social and academic fabric of the school is critical to young adult civic and political development because identification with and participation in a larger community is associated not only with civic engagement but also with political participation (Putnam 2000). For instance, in their review of the empirical literature, James Youniss, Jeffrey McLellan, and Miranda Yates (1997) found that, across studies, high school students involved in community service and school governance were significantly more likely to vote during young adulthood than their nonparticipatory peers. For adolescents, the community context of greatest potential impact and interest is often the high school.

High schools offer students pathways to social integration and a sense of connection to the institution by promoting schoolwide culture (for example, through sports events, school mascots, and other ways of enhancing school identity), fostering peer relations, and providing students with opportunities for extracurricular involvement and volunteer activities. As high school shapes students' social and academic experiences, a multitude of other school-related factors come into play: school policies and practices, the composition of the student body, and informal social processes. All these factors coalesce to produce the next generation of citizens.

A sense of belonging among adults influences their political engagement (Putnam 2000), and it is no less likely to shape young adults' political participation as well. In fact, using nationally representative data, Elizabeth Smith (1999) finds that a sense of belonging during adolescence, whether to school-oriented clubs and activities or to religious groups, is positively associated with early adult political participation. Developing peer and social communities and forging independent connections to formal social institutions outside the family are processes that begin in earnest in adolescence (Coleman 1990). A strong peer network provides adolescents with a sense of community, as does involvement with a team or a club. Likewise, volunteering to help those in need fosters in adolescents a sense of contributing to something larger than themselves.

During adolescence, youth begin to form individual and group identities as well as the ability to negotiate interpersonal relationships. Whether students develop an identity that is prosocial, academic, or civic may be related not only to the type of extracurricular activities they participate in but also to the school context (Eccles and Barber 1999; Eccles et al. 2003). For example, Daniel McFarland and Reuben Thomas (2006) find that high school students who volunteer and are involved in community service during high school are more likely to participate politically during young adulthood. It is likely that adolescents' integration into the social fabric of their high school and involvement in a variety of extracurricular activities are highly associated with their social and political involvement during young adulthood.

As is evident from this brief review, scholars have long argued that social as well as academic integration during adolescence shapes young adults' civic and political futures, but little research has explored how these processes work for the children of immigrants in particular. As a result, we know relatively little about the benefits or detriments of social integration for adolescent children of immigrants in the transition from high school to young adulthood. Our knowledge of the social integration of adolescent children of immigrants with their peers in comparison to children of native-born parents is equally limited.

Understanding the potential effects of the social aspects of school presents particular challenges. Students enter high school with defined interests and predispositions for social engagement. To argue that the high school has an *effect* implies that the effect would not take place, or would not take place in the same way, in the absence of the social aspect of the school experience. The complexity of the high school experience exacerbates the challenge of understanding the effects of its social aspects in that large U.S. high schools often offer many venues for adolescents to get involved and connect with the school. Furthermore, the academic and social structures of high schools are connected and reinforcing. Although we attempt to pinpoint the activities of adolescents and the forms of their social connections to their school, it is worth mentioning that adolescents also act as agents in that they choose their own avenues for social engagement, taking advantage of the opportunities provided by the high school.

These complexities notwithstanding, it has been found that social integration in high school via extracurricular involvement predicts political activity among young adults, even after accounting for political attitudes and personality traits (Glanville 1999). Despite the time commitment required, extracurricular involvement has been found to enhance academic achievement; Herbert Marsh (1992) theorizes that this effect may reflect a commitment to the formal institution of school and to school values. Such a link to an institution and the values of the institution may indirectly shape political participation in young adulthood.

Extracurricular activities can take various forms that are linked to later outcomes, from academic and arts clubs to student government and athletics (Broh 2002; McFarland and Thomas 2006). For example, Andrew Guest and Barbara Schneider (2003) illustrate that participation in non-athletic extracurricular activities consistently predicts positive academic outcomes whereas involvement in athletic activities does not. In addition, Jennifer Fredricks and Jacquelynne Eccles (2006) find that adolescent extracurricular involvement is associated with postsecondary civic engagement and political participation, even when taking prosocial activities into account. The regularity of extracurricular participation is another factor: students who consistently participate in at least one activity throughout high school are significantly more likely to vote than their peers who sporadically or never participate (Zaff et al. 2003). Not only the type of activities but also the depth and breadth of youths' extracurricular involvement may shape their future political participation. The connections that adolescents make to the institution of the school through extracurricular avenues lay the foundation for their civic and political connections to the community and to adult social institutions as they enter adulthood.

Among civic-oriented extracurricular activities, student government in particular is associated with future political participation and voting (Youniss et al. 1997). The positive relationship between participation in student government during high school and voting in early adulthood remains even after taking into account peer social integration, political interest and awareness, and self-efficacy (Glanville 1999). Likewise, even though parents' civic engagement influences their children's political participation in young adulthood, parental support for extracurricular involvement and civic engagement matters most when the parents themselves are not active in civic matters (Fletcher, Elder, and Mekos 2000). This may be especially relevant for children of immigrants, many of whom have parents who are working toward citizenship but are otherwise limited in their ability to participate politically. Although we still know relatively little about how extracurricular involvement shapes the civic development of children of immigrant parents, we hypothesize that, by definition, these children are more sensitive to the influence of extracurricular involvement on later political participation than children of native-born parents.

Research also links adolescents' participation in voluntary activities to later political participation, even when mediated by volunteering during young adulthood (Hanks 1981). Adolescent volunteering in particular predicts future political participation, as measured by civic engagement and voting (Youniss et al. 1997). Richard Niemi, Mary Hepburn, and Chris Chapman (2000) illustrate the relationship between volunteering and the formation of political and civic knowledge among adolescents; more specifically, McFarland and Thomas (2006) show that adolescent voluntary service that directly addresses social issues and assists those in need influences active civic engagement and political participation during young adulthood. In fact, both voluntary and mandatory community service, along with extracurricular involvement, have been found to predict voting and volunteering in young adulthood (Hart et al. 2007). It is important to note, however, that adolescents engage in voluntary activities made possible not only through their high schools but also through their churches and other religious organizations.

Adolescents' extracurricular involvement and volunteering reflect certain aspects of their individual social connections, both to formal organizations and to the institution of school. Social connection is also realized in one's sense of belonging to a community. Among adults, Robert Putnam (2000) emphasizes the importance of this sense of belonging to maintaining the civic fabric of society. Connection to a community and identification with a larger group are highly associated with civic engagement, especially as it relates to political participation (Delli Carpini 2000; Youniss et al. 1997). A feeling of belonging also facilitates political participation and civic engagement in young adulthood (Smith 1999). Putnam's work (2000) documents the loss of social connection in U.S. society and describes the impact of that loss on American civic engagement. The question of social connection and belonging is relevant to the future political participation of children of immigrants, who may find themselves academically and socially marginalized in U.S. high schools (Harklau 1994b; Katz 1999; Olsen 1997).

COLLEGE AND WORKFORCE PREPARATION: STRATIFICATION IN EDUCATION

Today our nation's young people stay in school longer than in the past and more of them work toward postsecondary degrees. Consequently, the period of late adolescence and early adulthood represents a time for exposure to a diversity of ideas, cultures, and understandings through experiences at school for more young people than ever before. Even for those who do not continue on into postsecondary study, however, the high school years, coming as they do immediately before adolescents have their first opportunity to vote, also represent a crucial point in their development.

Past research confirms a strong and positive association between academic achievement and political participation. Overall, scholars have found that college graduates are more likely to vote than those who do not complete college (Milligan, Morettib, and Oreopoulosc 2004). Among adolescents, overall high school achievement predicts political participation during young adulthood (Nie, Junn, and Stehlik-Barry 1996). In addition, enrollment in a high school whose students perform academically at relatively high levels may also influence the likelihood of political participation among its graduates.

Adolescents' schools and communities shape not only their social and professional identity and affiliation as young adults but also their early adult political behavior. The linguistic, ethnic, and immigrant composition of their school's student body may influence its dominant social norms, creating a school climate that more or less encourages the involvement of children of immigrants and their families in some of the same ways that ethnic enclave communities can promote political participation among adults (DeSipio 2002; Ramakrishnan and Bloemraad 2008). For example, a high-immigrant, linguistically diverse school may foster the civic incorporation of children of immigrants through native-language discussions and coethnic community building in ways that an English-dominant school that is predominantly white or African American simply cannot.

The high school years also represent a time when the opportunities for attaining education and socioeconomic status as an adult crystallize. Thus, the potential impact on early adult political engagement of experiences during this stage of life is heightened because of the strong linkage of socioeconomic status to adult political development (Coleman 1990; Phelan, Yu, and Davidson 1994). As a larger proportion of our population attends some type of postsecondary institution, postsecondary educational attainment is likely to define adults' socioeconomic position in society more than ever. One way in which high schools contribute to the political participation of young adults is through their role in shaping long-term educational disparities, because more highly educated people are more politically active.

Political and Civic Curriculum of Schools

Children of immigrants are typically more successful academically than their peers with similar social, economic, and racial backgrounds whose parents are native-born (Kao and Tienda 1995; Portes and MacLeod 1996), and several aspects of their academic experiences as they relate to the development of their political identity and interest in engagement are especially noteworthy.

First, the academic courses they take and their experiences in U.S. schools may contribute to the political engagement of adolescent children of immigrants more than happens with their peers whose parents are native-born if their school's focus on U.S. civic and political experiences complements the immigrant parents' experience with or knowledge of their native political systems. Second, if there is something about what students learn in school that contributes to political engagement—that is, if knowledge or skills gained in school, for example, through social science courses, rather than simply having a higher socioeconomic status is the reason why more highly educated individuals are more politically active—then children of immigrants may be more engaged in the learning that takes place in school and may reap more knowledge that encourages political participation, beyond what is reflected in their academic success. Third, because some children of immigrants—first-generation and recent immigrants in particular—may come to the U.S. social science classroom with a civic base developed in their home country, their prior educational experiences can be expected to shape their civic outcomes as well (Bratsberg and Ragan 2002; Ruiz-de-Velasco and Fix 2000). For these adolescents, high school social science coursework may present a unique entrée into U.S. civic society and an opportunity to compare and contrast in order to integrate into the host country.

All three of these aspects of social science course-taking and curriculum are represented in the word cloud we created from our teacher interviews (see figure 2.1). Early in the interviews, we asked our participating high school social science teachers to explain to us why they thought social science curriculum and course-taking are important for children of immigrants in particular. Teachers' answers ranged from the detailed and specific to the very holistic. Ultimately, however, the teachers all came back to the importance of teaching students to question, to interrogate new information, and to make connections to their lived experiences (that is, to "think," "understand," "question," and "know"). In addition, our social science teachers stressed the importance of students' political coming of age and their empowerment through the curriculum ("vote," "election," "democracy," "political process," "citizenship"), which teaches them to understand that they can effect social change and therefore conveys to them a sense of responsibility about their own future and the future of their communities. Some children of immigrants may receive their first exposure to concepts of American citizenship in the social science classroom, and after this first exposure, they can then further develop these concepts within their families and communities. Teachers and their immigrant students can work together to articulate and expand the students' potential in civic society as they transition into young adulthood.

Prior research exploring the rigor of academic coursework has clarified the relationship between overall academic achievement and political participation among young adults. We refine this argument by suggesting that social science achievement in particular is associated with future political participation. Indeed, civic instruction alone is related to factors such as political knowledge and trust (Atherton 2000). Building on this research, our work highlights academic achievement in the social sciences as a factor that may influence political participation in early adulthood, especially among the

Figure 2.1.   Word Cloud: Teachers' Answers to the Question "Why do you think social science matters for children of immigrants?"

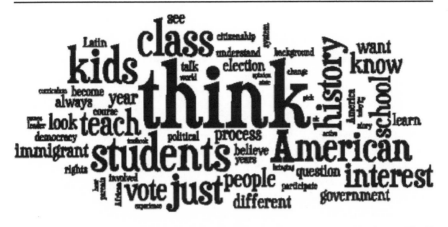

Source: Authors' calculation of New Citizens in a New Century data (Callahan 2008).

children of immigrants. The social science preparation that children of immigrants receive may shape their future political participation in ways that do not occur with children of native-born parents. Most foreign-born parents have less experience with the U.S. political system than native-born parents; consequently, schools and social science classes are more likely to provide a primary source of political knowledge and training for students to use in building on the political knowledge base that their immigrant parents brought with them from their home country.

Social science coursework also contributes to active political participation during young adulthood indirectly via heightened political awareness and knowledge (Atherton 2000; Chaffee 2000; Niemi and Junn 1998). Lonnie Sherrod (2003) finds that political knowledge during adolescence predicts voting and other behaviors during young adulthood and that this knowledge is gained, at least in part, through social science coursework. This coursework, designed to contribute to students' civic and political knowledge, may provide a critical source of information about U.S. society, especially for children of immigrant parents who may be relatively unfamiliar with U.S. social and political systems. William Galston (2001) articulates the role of civics coursework in producing political knowledge, which in turn shapes political participation, and he finds that enrollment in government and political science courses is especially important in developing the civic knowledge required for political participation during young adulthood. Richard Niemi and Julia Smith (2001) note that high school enrollment in government coursework has increased significantly over the past three decades, although

fewer students now enroll in either Advanced Placement (AP) or honors government coursework. Little is known, however, about how the social science
course-taking patterns of children of immigrants compare to those of children of native-born parents.

Conclusions

A wealth of research suggests that schools are powerful forces shaping adolescents' transitions to adulthood, both through formal academic preparation
and through organized and informal social settings and processes, but we also
know that schools differ from one another in a multitude of respects. They
offer different courses, their cultures and values vary, different extracurricular
activities are popular (and different ones are available), and status hierarchies
are not the same from one school to the next. High schools also differ in the
composition of their student bodies and their students' family backgrounds
and resources, as well as in teacher qualities, administration and policies, and
governance.

Traditionally, schools in which children of immigrants are enrolled have
been concentrated in relatively poor, urban, and high-minority areas compared to the schools attended by most children of native-born parents. However, with the most recent waves of immigration (Millard and Chapa 2004;
Wortham, Murillo, and Hamann 2002), many rural and suburban schools in
the Midwest and Southeast now face growing enrollments of children of immigrants with distinct linguistic and educational needs. Finally, schools and
districts vary in their approaches to many services, in no small part owing to
the needs of a given student body. Notable among the services that vary in
support and availability are primary language support (bilingual education)
and English as a Second Language (ESL) classes for students learning English.[1] Some of these differences can be captured with indicators from administrative databases, such as a school's passing rate on the state-mandated assessments or the percentage of teachers certified in a certain area of need,
such as ESL. However, many other features of the school cannot be easily
quantified. Schools may differ because of the unique characteristics of a principal, the local labor market for teachers, the involvement of parents, or some
other feature of their locale. Thus, the experiences of children of immigrants
are unlikely to be uniform but may have commonalities associated with their
school's need to respond to an immigrant population.

CHAPTER 3

Children of Immigrants and Their Schools

When children of immigrants walk through the doors of their high school, they enter a world with peers and teachers from different backgrounds and they experience the academic curriculum from a U.S. perspective. Their academic and social lives are shaped by shared courses, relationships with peers and teachers in the school, and participation in extracurricular clubs and other school activities. In crossing the school's threshold, children of immigrants enter a world that may be quite different from their family and neighborhood life.

A substantial body of literature has documented the development of family relationships among immigrant children in the United States (see, for example, Suárez-Orozco, Suárez-Orozco, and Todorova 2008). For children of immigrants, tension often arises from the clash between their families and the host culture when it comes to traditions, values, language, and way of life. In high school, children of immigrants acquire a life away from home, among typical U.S. teenagers, and their experiences of the home may come into conflict with their school lives among their peers. The journey for all adolescents as they transition into adulthood involves becoming independent from parents and family, but children of immigrants must balance their home and school cultures as they make this transition. From the vantage point of the school, however, adolescent children of immigrants may look in many respects like typical teenagers trying to navigate their way toward adulthood.

This chapter examines how immigrant teens fit into the social world of the school. We explore the connections of adolescent children of immigrants to their school along several dimensions, from language to social relationships and activities to, finally, their overall academic achievement. These social and academic connections set the stage for their integration into the institution of the school, which is a crucial step in developing their political identity and practices of political engagement.

Language: The Dominant Role of English-Language Proficiency

Prior research suggests that the majority of adolescent children of immigrants demonstrate not only a preference for English but relative proficiency in it

(Portes and Hao 1998), in many cases because they are either second-generation or 1.5-generation (those who arrived in the United States in the early elementary grades) (Portes and Rumbaut 2001; Rumbaut and Portes 2001). Most adolescent children of immigrants have been educated primarily in the U.S. school system; only a relatively small proportion are considered recent immigrants—that is, first-generation students who arrived within the past three to five years (Green et al. 2008; Ruiz-de-Velasco and Fix 2000; White and Glick 2000). The children of immigrants who come to the attention of educators are so-called language minorities—those whose first language is not English. However, language minority children of immigrants are extremely heterogeneous with respect to their English proficiency.

The development of English proficiency among children of immigrants has long been considered a critical measure of immigrant assimilation into U.S. society, even though prior to World War I many, if not most, immigrant communities provided schools for their children in the native language of the community (Kloss 1977; Wiley 2007). The onset of compulsory education during the isolationist period between World War I and World War II heightened the public perception of schools as America's melting pot (Greer 1969) and as primarily responsible, in this role, for teaching English to children of immigrants. It was not until after the civil rights era that other aspects of the education of language minority children of immigrants began to receive educational policy consideration.

In 1974 the education of Kinney Lau, a Chinese-descent English learner (EL) student in the San Francisco public schools, came under consideration by the Ninth Circuit Court of Appeals (Lau v. Nichols 1974). Lawyers argued that the school district did not offer ELs—language minority students not yet fully proficient in English—access to either English development or the core curriculum, in violation of the 1964 Civil Rights Act (Hakuta 2011). The court agreed, ruling that providing the same instruction to students learning English that their native-English-speaking classmates received was insufficient to ensure that EL students both learned English *and* mastered math, science, and history. With Lau, the court ruled that educators and schools would have to do more to ensure that Kinney and other EL students could succeed; however, the court specifically did not mandate classroom pedagogy in its decision. In theory, educational policy recognizes the importance of not only teaching English to the children of immigrants but also preparing them academically. Translating the spirit of the Lau decision into actual classroom practice, however, remains a point of contention.

Currently, most schools and districts comply with state and federal guidelines developed in response to and in compliance with the Lau decision by determining whether students are ELs or limited English proficient (LEP) and then, having identified the students in need of linguistic support services, placing them in language instruction classes (Hakuta 2011; Olsen 1995). The most common form of linguistic support services, especially at the secondary level, is coursework in English as a second language (ESL) (Zehler et al. 2003). Only when linguistic support services are securely in place can content area enrollment begin (Harklau 1994b; Minicucci and Olsen 1992). In addition, educators themselves may perceive English proficiency to be an academic gatekeeper for immigrant students (Harklau 1994a; Minicucci and Olsen 1993). Taken together, the dual roles of school—to provide language instruction and to prepare students academically in core subject areas for civic and labor market participation—may conflict through the logistics of student scheduling and school operations.

In turn, proficiency in English is among the factors most highly associated with children of immigrants' academic and social experiences. The Lau decision and other educational policies regarding language acquisition continue to shape the education of immigrant language minority youth based on measures of their English-language proficiency. Prior research suggests that linguistic rather than immigrant status is associated with academic placement and preparation for immigrant language minority youth (Callahan and Shiffrer 2012; Callahan, Wilkinson, and Muller 2010). The following section explores the academic and social school experiences of immigrant and native-born youth accordingly.

Schools and educators are often more aware of their students' linguistic status than of any number of other characteristics that might define the student, such as their economic status or their social, ethnic, or racial identity. In the dominant discourse of the school, proficiency in English tends to rise to the top as one of the most important language issues, if not *the* most important. Teachers of immigrant youth often recognize the salient role of the native language, however, in shaping not only educational outcomes (Bankston and Zhou 1995; Stanton-Salazar and Dornbusch 1995) but also students' experiences and position in the community (Portes and Rumbaut 2006). For instance, Ms. Foster, a New York government teacher, remarked on the importance of language in defining children of immigrants' position not only in their homes and their communities but also within the larger dominant culture:

> I've definitely had some students . . . with strong family bonds. I've met a lot of families where there were really strong bonds in the Latino community . . . but often [in school] there was this gap and disconnect in the language barrier. The student may have been the one that's translating, and [they] definitely live in both worlds. There's this gap for them trying to figure out how to move forward for themselves—an identity crisis, right?

Language proves to be one of the most salient, if not most visible, features with which children of immigrants define their adolescent identities. Which language to speak to whom? Teachers require English for the most part, but classmates and peers may not. With peers, language choices can either limit or expand an adolescent's network. Siblings' choice of language to use together also makes a statement about who they are and how they see themselves. Choosing to use the native language with their parents or choosing to use English will also shape adolescents' relationship with their parents into the future. Language shapes *who* the children of immigrant parents are, not only in the home and in the community but in the school as well.

Although parents often maintain good relationships with their children during the adolescent years, the forms of their involvement with the school often shift with the increasing independence and changing needs of their adolescents (McNeal 1999). Parents of struggling teens may still communicate with the school about academic or disciplinary matters, while other involved parents concentrate on attendance at schoolwide events, such as sports events or other programs (Muller 1993). Language minority status may widen the divide between home and school for some children of immigrants, however, because language minority parents tend to attend fewer such events and to be more reluctant to interact with or make requests of school administrators and teachers on behalf of their children (De Gaetano 2007; Huss-Keeler 1997). Thus, because many adolescent children of immigrants speak another language at home, language minority status has important implications for the involvement of their parents in the school. Immigrant generation status is also very important: a much higher proportion of first-generation immigrants grew up in non-native-English-speaking families compared to adolescents who were born in the United States. Figure 3.1 shows the language minority status of tenth-graders surveyed in 2002 in the Education Longitudinal Study by whether they were first-, second-, or third-plus-generation immigrants. Over three-quarters of first-generation students were non-native-English speakers, compared to only 2 percent of third-plus-generation teens. Second-generation immigrants fell somewhere in between: 44.5 percent were non-native-English speakers.

In addition, non-native-English-speaking adolescents differed in how often and under what circumstances they used their native language. Not surprisingly, many language minority adolescents spoke with their mothers in their native language exclusively. Figure 3.2 shows the frequency of native language use between the adolescent and his or her mother, by the student's generational status. Almost 70 percent of first-generation non-native-English-speaking adolescents spoke with their mother exclusively in their native language, compared to only 22 percent of third-generation non-native-English speakers. Second-generation students were somewhere between their first- and third-generation peers (but closer to those of the first generation): 57 percent spoke to their mother in their native language exclusively. We found a similar trend for adolescents' relationships with their fa-

Figure 3.1.   Language Minority Tenth-Graders, by Generational Status, 2002

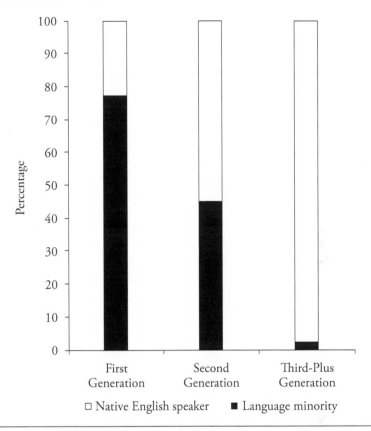

Source: Authors' tabulation of data from the Education Longitudinal Study, 2002 (Ingels et al. 2004).

thers (not shown). As might be expected, when it comes to native language use between parent and adolescent, the parent's immigrant status appears to be important.

Adolescents' relationships with their siblings may provide a bridge between family and school. Figure 3.3 shows the frequency of language use with siblings. Whereas only 35 percent of first-generation students always spoke with their siblings in their native language, even fewer second- and third-generation students did so. Interestingly, there is no discernible difference in language use between second- and third-generation siblings. It is possible that siblings' ages—and in particular whether they are school-age—determine the language they speak with each other (Duursma et al. 2007); Education Longitudinal Study (ELS) does not measure these factors.

Figure 3.2.   Language Minority Adolescents Speaking the Native Language
with Their Mother, by Generational Status and Frequency of Use,
2002

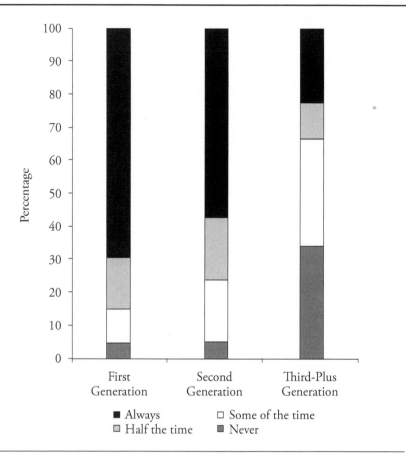

Source: Authors' tabulation of data from the Education Longitudinal Study, 2002 (Ingels et al. 2004).

Language use between non-native-English speakers and their friends, as shown in figure 3.4, illustrates the divide between family and friends for children of immigrants. In contrast to their native-language usage with family members, adolescents typically spoke English with their friends, and their immigrant generational status made little difference in this pattern. Few students spoke with friends in their native language exclusively; rather, the distinction in non-native-language usage among friends lay in whether they *ever* spoke a language other than English. Although we do not know from the ELS questions whether the surveyed relationships with peers were confined

Figure 3.3. Language Minority Adolescents Speaking the Native Language
with Siblings, by Generational Status and Frequency of Use, 2002

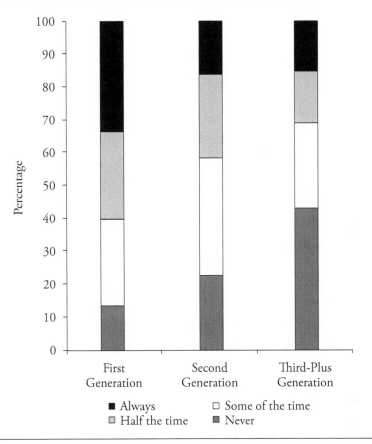

Source: Authors' tabulation of data from the Education Longitudinal Study, 2002 (Ingels et al. 2004).

to the school setting, it is reasonable to assume that the use of English among friends as compared to family members followed the lines of home and school boundaries, at least in part.

Peers and Social Connections

The schools that adolescent children of immigrants attend are social worlds in which the relationships between adolescents, their peers, and the adults who work in the school are varied and complex. The adolescent society of a school is structured and shaped by shared courses and extracurricular activities, as well as by the backgrounds, interests, and values of the individuals. It

Figure 3.4.   Language Minority Adolescents Speaking the Native Language with Friends, by Generational Status and Frequency of Use, 2002

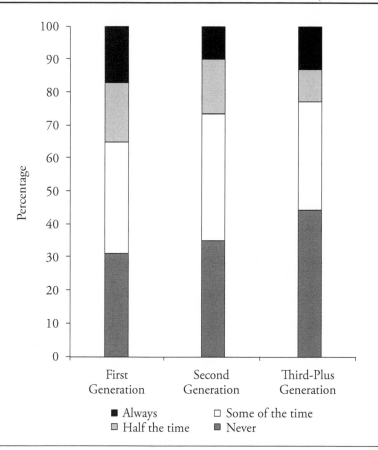

Source: Authors' tabulation of data from the Education Longitudinal Study, 2002 (Ingels et al. 2004).

is a community with boundaries, and students and teachers know and understand the boundaries, which are defined in both time (the school year, the four years of high school) and space (the building and the official functions of the school). Within these school boundaries are the venues that shape adolescents' cognitive and social development and from which relationships emerge. Adolescents seek friendships with those around them, whether through one-on-one interaction or through groups and cliques, and schools provide them not only with a venue for their social lives but also with pools of potential friends. (Indeed, the persuasive power of adolescents who are potential friends may be greater than that of actual friends; see Giordano

2003.) In this setting, the developing adolescent comes to understand self in relation to others, gaining a sense of identity and making choices that carry over into adulthood (Akerlof and Kranton 2002; Frank et al. 2008). How does the immigrant student fit into this complex scenario? We begin to answer this question by examining adolescent children of immigrants in their extracurricular activities and in their relations with peers and teachers.

EXTRACURRICULAR INVOLVEMENT

The typical U.S. high school offers students opportunities for structured extracurricular activities ranging from competitive team sports to hobby clubs and academic honor societies. Although most high schools have sports teams and honor societies, schools also offer clubs that reflect the interests and opportunities of the community served by the school. Thus, the extracurricular activities that students choose depend, in part, on the school they attend. A survey of selected yearbooks from the National Longitudinal Study of Adolescent Health (Add Health) schools revealed a wide range of clubs:

Color guard	Drama club	Track (boys)
AP economics	TV anchors	Stop AIDS for Everyone
Step team	Thespians	(SAFE)
Flaggies	TV crew	Track (girls)
Honor Humanitas	Stage crew	Rec club
Debate team	Varsity basketball (girls)	Filipino Club
Band	Fellowship of Christian	Homecoming court
Regular Humanitas	Athletes	Equestrian club
Mock trial team	General chorus	Latino Club
Drill team	Stats crew	Literary magazine
Decathlon	JV basketball (girls)	Peer counselors
Forensics team	Chamber singers	Black Heritage
Banner (Flag Corps)	Junior council	School newspaper
Journalism	Volleyball (girls)	FOCUS (support
National Art Honor	Madrigals	group)
Society	Leadership	Asian Pacific American
Junior varsity (JV)	Tennis (girls)	Club
cheerleading	Concert band	It's Academic
Journalism editors	Senior council	Mentoring program
French Honor Society	Tennis (boys)	AP calculus
Cheerleading	Yearbook	Math team
Football	Bible Club	SRO (stage orchestra)
Spanish Honor Society	Soccer	AP art
Songs	Best Buddies Club	Teen Republicans
National Honor Society	African American Club	Jazz band

AP English	SHOP (alcohol- and	Students Against Drunk
Marching band	drug-free environ-	Driving (SADD)
Orchestra	ment)	State Scholarship
AP history	Pugwash (application of	Federation
Imagemakers	science to technology)	

As is apparent from this list, the actual extracurricular activities in each school were diverse. Some school groups were academic in orientation: honor societies (for example, State Scholarship Federation, National Honor Society, National Art Honor Society), a variety of academically oriented activities (drama, speech and debate, choir, band and orchestra, journalism, math and science clubs, student government), and (in some schools) Advanced Placement (AP) groups (calculus, art, English, history). Other activities were sports-related, including both sports teams (football, basketball, track and field) and the pep units that provide support at sports events (cheerleaders, drill team, color guard, flag team, song leaders). All of the high schools whose yearbooks we examined provided students with various options for participating in the kind of sports and academic clubs that are characteristic of extracurricular activities at many high schools across the nation and generally attract the lion's share of participation (McFarland and Thomas 2006). Our review also shows, however, that it was common to find multiple venues for extracurricular involvement and engagement beyond academics and athletics.

These other extracurricular groups may have reflected cultures within the school. For example, we found that some schools had groups that were racial or ethnic in nature, such as Asian Pacific American Club, Filipino Club, Latino Club, and Black Heritage. Ethnic and cross-cultural groups may provide a particularly appealing social inroad for immigrant adolescents. In fact, as Mr. Jones, a U.S. history teacher in Florida, remarked, involvement in multicultural extracurricular groups is important for children of immigrants:

> At our school we have an organization called PRIDE that a large number of both white and Hispanic students are involved in. . . . Basically it is a multicultural extracurricular club. They get together a couple of times a month to talk about the issues. They raise money, and they do charitable work in the community. . . . That certainly facilitates a participation in the political process and fosters a very positive [*unintelligible*] image for other students.

It is not just the topic around which the group meets but also the format of the group that can provide a welcoming environment for immigrant youth and allow them to safely connect with sympathetic-minded friends from the dominant culture.

Other groups were organized around community service, both programs that provided services within the school, such as mentoring and peer counseling programs, and organizations that worked outside the school, such as Best Buddies, Students Against Drunk Driving (SADD), and Stop AIDS for Everyone (SAFE). Religious organizations in high schools overlapped with community service organizations and were likely to reflect the larger community of the high school (for example, Fellowship of Christian Athletes, Bible Club). And finally, some clubs were what could be considered recreational or hobbyist in nature, such as chess club or photography club.

Collectively, participation in such organizations and activities gives a student the opportunity to define his or her identity and interact with others with similar interests. These activities, which generally take place outside of the classroom setting, may also provide a venue in which they can meet students in other grade levels. It is worth noting, however, that not all students participate in extracurricular activities: assuming that those who appeared only in the mug shots section of the yearbook had no extracurricular involvements, we conclude that roughly half of the students in the schools from our yearbook study did not participate in extracurricular activities. Other students appeared on as many as ten separate pages of their yearbook. We found no trend in the number of extracurricular activities offered according to the number of children of immigrants who attended the school, although the particular offerings clearly reflected the student body composition.

High school extracurricular activities are usually sponsored by a teacher or other adult professional from the school. Clubs offer students opportunities for leadership as team captains and as upperclassmen mentoring lowerclassmen, as well as for interaction with other students and teachers they do not usually have contact with in their classes. Some clubs involve travel, especially teams and clubs involved in playoffs and competitions, and many help students broaden their understanding and experience through hands-on involvement in the community, whether through volunteer work or car washes, bake sales, and other fund-raising events. In other words, through teams and voluntary associations, extracurricular activities connect the student not only to the institution of the school but also to the world of institutional affiliation (Frisco, Muller, and Dodson 2004; Wuthnow 1997). Taken together, these effects of extracurricular participation during the high school years help students develop the kind of identity and affiliation that lead to civic and political participation in early adulthood (McFarland and Thomas 2006; Zaff et al. 2003). Thus, students' extracurricular involvement during high school may shape multiple facets of their lives in young adulthood.

In general, immigrant high school students and native-born students participate in extracurricular activities in similar ways, except that children of immigrants participate at slightly lower rates. This lower level of participation may be due to limited extracurricular offerings at many of the immigrant-majority schools, which also tend to be relatively low-income and high-minority. However, children of immigrants' somewhat lower levels of extra-curricular involvement may also reflect their relative lack of freedom to engage in after-school activities, given many of the social and economic constraints faced by their families. Nevertheless, the trends in the participation of children of immigrants in extracurricular activities largely mirror the trends in participation among children of native-born parents.

Table 3.1 shows self-reported participation rates from two different data sets, Add Health and ELS, by type of activity. Children of immigrants' significantly lower rate of overall extracurricular participation is due mainly to their limited involvement in sports and fine arts. Indeed, children of immigrants even participated less in soccer, a sport more popular in countries outside the United States. On the other hand, children of immigrants participated more often in academic clubs, consistent with their well-documented academic success. We found no evidence of significant differences in politically focused extracurricular involvement; immigrant youth participated in student council at levels comparable to those of their third-plus-generation peers.

In contrast to their extracurricular participation, children of immigrants reported volunteering during high school at greater rates than their third-plus-generation peers in both Add Health and ELS. The careful reader will note the stark differences in reported volunteering rates between Add Health (47 percent among children of immigrants and 43 percent among children of native-born parents) and ELS (16 percent and 13 percent, respectively); this difference is probably due to the phrasing of the survey items. In wave 3, Add Health respondents were asked retrospectively if they *ever* volunteered during high school; in contrast, ELS students were asked if they participated in school-based volunteering—to the exclusion of religious and other community-based voluntary activities. These results are consistent with—and may be related to—the higher rates of religious involvement among children of immigrants.

In fact, many of the Latino young adults in our qualitative inquiry not only cited volunteering as having connected them to their community but also gave it credit for helping to shape their civic perspective. Many began volunteering through their religious institution to fulfill a school community service requirement, but continued even after they had fulfilled the requirement. Rafael from Florida noted that he "did a little bit of church work [to fulfill] the requirement of community service hours . . . and then I did a little bit extra. . . . I definitely became more involved in the community." Whether or not the volunteering was initially mandatory, many of our respondents reported that these experiences made them reconsider their place in society. Genaro, a New Yorker of Cuban-Dominican origin, said:

> You feel a certain emotion when you're helping out people . . . it's kind of gratifying and a little selfish helping out people. I can admit that. I'm being

Table 3.1 Proportions of Children of Immigrants and Children of Native-Born Parents Who Participate in Extracurricular and Volunteering Activities, 1994–2001 and 2002

	Add Health			ELS		
	Children of Immigrants (N = 1,883)	Children of Native-Born (N = 10,964)	Significant Difference	Children of Immigrants (N = 2,527)	Children of Native-Born (N = 9,232)	Significant Difference
Any extracurricular	0.81	0.85	***	0.74	0.86	***
Sport	0.52	0.59	***	0.57	0.71	***
Academic club	0.20	0.16	***	0.14	0.15	
Student council	0.07	0.08		0.06	0.08	***
Fine arts	0.20	0.28	***			
Volunteering	0.47	0.43		0.16	0.13	***

Source: Add Health (Bearman et al. 1997) and Education Longitudinal Study (Ingels et al. 2004). In Add Health, fine arts covers orchestra and drama and academics covers computer, debate, history, and math. In the ELS any academic club includes academic honor societies and academic clubs, and intramurals are included in "any sport."

*** $p \leq .001$

selfish when I help people. When I help people, it's more about like I have to. This is something that I have to do in order to complete me. Because if I don't do this, then I'm not who I am. You get what I'm saying? It's who I am. I have to help.

The social and civic integration that children of immigrants experience in their volunteering activities strengthens their civic bonds (Putnam 2000). Once they become connected to other social groups and embedded in others' lives, these immigrant young adults find that it is important to play a citizen's role in their community.

Friends: Children of Immigrants and Children of Native-Born Parents

The Add Health data set provides a unique opportunity to examine characteristics of students' school-based friendships. Table 3.2 shows characteristics of students' friends by whether the friend was the child of immigrant or native-born parents. Not surprisingly, like the adolescent children of immigrants themselves, their friends were more likely to live in language minority families where a language other than English was spoken. Similarly, adolescent children of immigrants had a higher proportion of friends who were also immigrants. Although relatively few high school students were placed in ESL, about 3 percent of children of immigrants had friends in ESL courses, compared to 0 percent among the third-plus-generation students.[1] These patterns may be partly a function of the composition of schools: many children of immigrants attend schools with high concentrations of immigrant youth. In addition, adolescent children of immigrants are more likely than children of native-born parents to form friendships with peers who value education and expect to go to college. Schools also differ in the extent to which students

Table 3.2   Characteristics of Friends of Children of Immigrants and Children of Native-Born Parents: Means and Proportions, 1994–2001

	Children of Immigrants (N = 3,369)	Children of Native-Born (N = 12,246)	Significant Difference
Language minority	0.19	0.01	***
ESL student	0.03	0.00	*
Immigrant	0.43	0.08	***
Expects to go to college	4.23	4.28	

Source: Add Health (Bearman et al. 1997) and AHAA (Muller et al. 2007).
*$p \leq .05$; ***$p \leq .001$

in ESL coursework are isolated from students in other academic courses (Callahan et al. 2009). Such segregation by immigrant status may have contributed to the observed differences in friendship patterns. Interestingly, the friends of children of immigrants were neither more nor less likely to expect to go to college than the friends of children of native-born parents.

Academic Orientation: Attitudes About Education, School, and Teachers

Much has been made about optimism among children of immigrants (Kao and Tienda 1995; Perreira, Harris, and Dohoon 2006; Rosenbaum and Rochford 2008). The immigrant optimism theory posits that immigrant students tend to work harder and value school more than children of native-born parents. Using both Add Health and ELS, we explore the educational expectations and aspirations of children of immigrants, the educational attitudes held by their friends, and their sense of support from and connection to school and teachers (see table 3.3).

We know that adults' social integration into and connection with the larger community is linked to their civic integration and participation (Putnam 2000), but whether and how the social connection of adolescents to their school community is related to their future political and civic participation is open to consideration. Because adolescents spend many of their waking hours in school, the school environment may outweigh the neighborhood environment in shaping their future political engagement.[2] It is within the context of the school that adolescents begin to develop a sense of community and social connection outside of the home and the family. In table 3.3, we compare the overall social connection of immigrant youth and their third-plus-generation peers to their school. Students felt equally connected socially overall, regardless of immigrant status. Although third-plus-generation students were significantly more likely to report feeling a part of their school, immigrant youth reported feeling significantly happier at school and liking it more, and they also reported a greater attachment to their teachers. Consistent with this positive sentiment, children of immigrants were significantly less likely to feel that students in the school were prejudiced, and they reported working harder in school.

Children of immigrants reported higher educational aspirations (using Add Health), but lower educational expectations (using ELS) relative to children of native-born parents. We found slightly inconsistent results between the Add Health and ELS data sets, possibly owing to differences in the wording of survey items ("How much do you *want to* go to college?" versus "How far in school do you *think* you will go?"). In multivariate models (not shown), holding social background constant, we found that children of immigrants

Table 3.3 Students' Attitudes About School and Teachers, Including Their College Aspirations and Expectations: Means and Proportions, 1994–2001 and 2004

	Add Health			ELS		
	Children of Immigrants (N = 4,186)	Children of Native-Born (N = 14,508)	Significant Difference	Children of Immigrants (N = 2,530)	Children of Native-Born (N = 9,164)	Significant Difference
Teacher attachment	3.82	3.69	***	2.03	2.12	**
Happy at school	3.78	3.67	***			
Feels part of school	3.73	3.85	***			
Feels close to people at school	3.70	3.70				
Social connection	3.74	3.74				
Students are prejudiced	3.02	3.17	***			
Student reports working hard in school				2.79	2.69	***
Student reports liking school				2.22	2.10	***
College aspirations	0.85	0.82	**	0.81	0.82	
College expectations	0.76	0.74		0.65	0.68	*

Source: Add Health (Bearman et al. 1997) and Education Longitudinal Study (Ingels et al. 2004).
*p ≤ .05; **p ≤ .01; ***p ≤ .001

reported higher educational aspirations and expectations than children of native-born parents.

For the most part, however, we found that children of immigrants and their non-immigrant peers experience the social and relational aspects of high school, and of adolescence generally, in similar ways. Despite these commonalities, informal school processes are only one piece of the high school experience. In the following chapter, we explore the academic preparation and achievement of adolescents, both children of immigrants and children of native-born parents.

CHAPTER 4

Academic Opportunity and Stratification Among Children of Immigrants and Children of Native-Born Parents

We hypothesize that American high schools shape future political participation through two primary pathways. First, high schools stratify students, sorting and ranking them into courses at different levels, with different demands, and assigning indicators, like grades, of academic performance and college readiness. Such stratification contributes directly to students' educational attainment and adult socioeconomic status, which is one of the best-documented educational determinants of voting (Brady et al. 1995). Second, high school social science coursework is designed to teach students how the U.S. political system functions; the roles of voters, stakeholders, and advocates in a democracy; the three branches of government; and the tenets of the U.S. Constitution. This chapter examines the foundation of the first mechanism, the stratification of students, as it pertains to school processes. In particular, we consider the overall academic achievement and attainment of immigrant youth relative to the children of native-born parents as a precursor to their future political participation.

Academic success, as indicated by adolescents' grades, course-taking, and attainment, is an important determinant of long-run socioeconomic outcomes. Students who leave high school with relatively high levels of academic preparation are more likely to attend and complete college. In turn, individuals with higher levels of educational attainment are more likely to vote. Similarly, higher levels of education open the doors to higher-paying professional opportunities, and again, higher SES is associated with a greater likelihood of political participation.

Although the relationship between SES and voting is well recognized, it is less well understood in terms of both how it works and whether it contributes to a democracy that represents the interests of all members of the population. Generally, a number of factors are likely to contribute to the proclivity of those with higher SES to vote. Individuals with higher levels of education and better jobs generally enjoy stronger connections to institutions in general

(Hart et al. 2007), have a relatively greater sense of individual agency (Youniss et al. 1997), derive greater benefits from voting relative to the personal cost (Downs 1957), and maintain higher levels of overall political engagement (Verba, Schlozman, and Brady 1996). Whether this pattern contributes to greater overall stratification (Junn 1999) or leads to a system in which those who vote are better informed and have higher skill levels (Cho 1999) is debatable.

In fact, in her seminal work on (non)voting among immigrants, Wendy Cho (1999) argues that socioeconomic status is a necessary, yet insufficient predictor of future political participation. In particular, she points to the role of socialization as measured by length of time in the United States as a key factor shaping immigrants' political participation. In models that control on nativity and English proficiency, she finds that the significance of race and ethnicity in predicting voting behavior disappears completely. Thus, Cho argues, while social class may be a primary predictor of voting among the majority population, socialization holds greater sway among the foreign-born population. Similarly, Karthick Ramakrishnan (2005) argues that while race-ethnicity and social class matter in predicting political outcomes, among immigrant populations it is also true that generational status and time in the United States—education and acculturation—are critical. Citizenship itself does not ensure the political participation of immigrants; even after gaining their citizenship, socialization remains central to their political involvement.

These studies are based on immigrants in the general population. In this chapter, our concentration on adolescent children of immigrants who attended U.S. schools allows us to highlight a central aspect of the socialization of children of immigrants—educational preparation in the high school. For children of native-born and immigrants alike, how they are educated, treated, and trained within the halls and classrooms of U.S. high schools shapes their trajectories—including their future political participation.

The Opportunity to Learn in U.S. High Schools

Although most schools no longer officially "track" students, the fact remains that not all courses are created equal: some prepare adolescents for further education, while others prepare them to graduate from high school. State-level graduation requirements may fall far below the minimum coursework necessary to apply for entry into a four-year university (Schiller and Muller 2003). For example, even if a student takes three years of math in high school, if she does not complete algebra II, she remains ill prepared for entry into a four-year university. Similarly, a student may complete two or even three years of social science coursework, but if none of the courses are honors or AP level, he is likely to face additional challenges in a four-year college.

As discussed in the introduction to this book, a rich body of work documents the academic experiences of children of immigrants in U.S. high schools and, overall, paints a portrait of educational inequality and limited access (Hao and Pong 2008; Portes and Fernandez-Kelly 2008; Rumbaut and Portes 2001; Stone and Han 2005). Since higher educational attainment probably makes a major contribution to voting behavior across the life course, it is helpful to better understand some of the structural and systemic mechanisms in schools that shape the educational experiences of children of immigrants.

Although, as we demonstrated in chapter 3, the social experiences in high school of children of immigrants are remarkably similar to those of children of native-born parents, the former are disproportionately enrolled in both schools and courses of relatively poor academic quality (Callahan et al. 2009; Portes and Hao 2004; Zuniga, Olson, and Winter 2005). One of the mechanisms shaping the educational experiences of children of immigrants may be the academic stratification discussed in chapter 1 (Gamoran 1987, 2001; Lucas 1999; Oakes 1985). In particular, as non-native English speakers, many children of immigrants are identified for placement in linguistic support services, such as English as a second language (ESL) coursework. Not all children of immigrants are identified for such placement, but among those who are, ESL may be a school-based mechanism that shapes their academic trajectories.

EDUCATIONAL PERFORMANCE AND PREPARATION

Although the high school graduation rates of children of immigrants are not as high as those of their third-plus-generation peers (Kalogrides 2009; Valenzuela 1999), research suggests that once background characteristics are taken into account, immigrant youth in fact are significantly more likely to graduate (Perreira et al. 2006; White and Glick 2000). In fact, in certain contexts, such as Catholic schools, children of immigrants graduate at rates on par with those of children of native-born parents (Louie and Holdaway 2009). Similarly, children of immigrants are less likely to enroll in higher education than children of native-born parents (Fry 2002; Hagy and Staniec 2002; Keller and Tillman 2008); an immigrant advantage emerges only when background characteristics are taken into account.

Grades and Test Scores Likewise, scholars have noted that while immigrant youth tend to earn lower grades and test scores than the third-plus generation, this difference disappears once background is taken into account (Glick and White 2003; Pong and Hao 2007). Lingxin Hao and Suet-ling Pong (2008) find that the postsecondary attainment of first-generation immigrant young adults is higher than that of their native-born peers, even after their background, high school performance, and preparation are taken into account. Patterns of academic performance among children of immigrants have been explored through applications of segmented assimilation theory (Portes and Fernandez-Kelly 2008; Rumbaut 1994; Zhou 1997b) and the immigrant optimism hypothesis (Kao and Tienda 1995).

Course-Taking and Preparation for College   Our prior research suggests that immigrants' academic performance patterns draw from their high school experience with academic preparation (Callahan et al. 2010; Callahan et al. 2009). High school course-taking prepares students not only for graduation and the labor force but also for college-going. Completion of math coursework in particular is highly predictive of enrollment in a four-year university (Adelman 1999), so much so that math placement can serve as a proxy for college preparatory course-taking. Similarly, enrollment in honors, Advanced Placement (AP), or international baccalaureate (IB) social science courses can distinguish general education coursework from college preparatory coursework.

Table 4.1 presents the means and standard deviations for two measures of high school academic performance—grades earned (math, social science, and overall GPA) and math and social science course-taking—by immigrant status, using both Add Health and ELS data. As the table demonstrates, children of immigrants in the ELS database showed significantly lower levels of academic performance than children of native-born parents ($p < .01$). In fact, just over two-thirds of children of immigrants completed college preparatory math coursework—algebra II or higher—by the end of high school, compared to nearly three-fourths of children of native-born parents. On average, children of immigrants earned 0.15 of a grade point lower in their overall grade point average and in their math and social science course grades. Comparing Asian and Latino student performance, however, we see that the mean course-taking and grades earned among children of immigrants were driven by the performance of the relatively large Latino subgroup. Remember that there is a great deal of variation within each of these pan-ethnic groupings: the Japanese and Hmong immigrant experiences differ markedly from one another, as do those of Cubans and Hondurans. Ideally, we would explore patterns by national origin, but the relative sample sizes preclude us from doing so. In reflecting on the differences in pan-ethnic group performance, it is thus critical to keep the heterogeneity of each group in mind.

Clear trends emerged when we parsed the Latino and Asian patterns of grades and course-taking. In the Education Longitudinal Study, only 60 percent of Latino children of immigrants—compared to 84 percent of Asian children of immigrants—completed algebra II prior to the end of high school. Asian immigrant students disproportionately completed advanced math or higher by the end of high school, while on average Latino immigrant students disproportionately completed the math curriculum only through

Table 4.1   High School Academic Achievement and Attainment, by Immigrant Status: Proportions, Means, and Standard Deviations for Averages, 1994–2001 and 2004

				Course-Taking			
	N	Highest Math[ab]	Standard Deviation	Algebra II or Higher	Social Science Credits[ab]	Standard Deviation	College Prep Social Science[b]
Add Health							
Children of immigrants	2,445	6.34	(1.64)	0.67	3.44	(1.10)	0.34
Latino	1,198	5.67	(1.48)	0.53	3.19	(1.19)	0.27
Asian	734	7.19	(1.30)	0.83	3.53	(0.75)	0.41
Children of native-born	9,128	6.03	(2.04)	0.62	3.55	(1.44)	0.26
Latino	599	5.63	(1.75)	0.51	3.16	(1.38)	0.24
Asian	166	6.26	(1.42)	0.66	4.07	(0.81)	0.23
ELS							
Children of immigrants	2,992	6.45	(1.64)	0.68	3.54	(1.15)	0.25
Latino	727	6.07	1.72	0.60	3.36	1.28	0.19
Asian	996	7.34	1.09	0.84	3.66	0.78	0.42
Children of native-born	8,792	6.55	1.84	0.73	3.75	1.29	0.23
Latino	581	6.07	1.79	0.63	3.47	1.33	0.12
Asian	65	6.64	1.86	0.63	3.67	1.24	0.25

Source: Add Health (Bearman et al. 1997), AHAA (Muller et al. 2007), and Education Longitudinal Study (Ingels et al. 2004).
[a]Differences in means between children of immigrant and native-born parents are significant at $p \leq .01$ or less in the ELS data set.
[b]Differences in means between children of immigrant and native-born parents are significant at $p \leq .01$ or less in the Add Health data set.

geometry, which is below the recommended threshold for college preparation (Adelman 2006). We see similar patterns in the number of social science credits completed by students. On average, children of both immigrant and native-born parents completed around three and a half years of social science coursework prior to the end of high school, and Asians completed about one-third of a semester more social science coursework than Latinos.

Subgroup differences in the Add Health data are less pronounced, although we again found evidence of disparities in performance by the Latino and Asian immigrant subgroups. In the Add Health data set, children of im-

		Academic Performance			
Overall GPA[a]	Standard Deviation	Math GPA[a]	Standard Deviation	Social Science GPA[a]	Standard Deviation
2.57	(0.71)	2.20	(0.80)	2.47	(0.82)
2.30	(0.68)	1.90	(0.73)	2.17	(0.81)
2.91	(0.56)	2.60	(0.71)	2.82	(0.64)
2.55	(0.89)	2.18	(1.00)	2.45	(1.05)
2.28	(0.77)	1.88	(0.85)	2.13	(0.92)
2.70	(0.54)	2.32	(0.56)	2.63	(0.59)
2.59	(0.72)	1.89	(0.86)	2.47	(0.88)
2.41	0.78	1.69	0.90	2.27	0.97
2.98	0.47	2.36	0.58	2.89	2.77
2.74	2.83	2.03	0.94	2.61	0.98
2.48	0.75	1.77	0.87	2.35	0.94
2.82	0.73	2.16	0.84	2.77	0.86

migrants took significantly fewer social science credits and did significantly more math coursework than did children of native-born parents. This relationship was driven by the relatively high math course-taking of the Asian immigrant subgroup. As mentioned earlier, on average Asian children of immigrants completed advanced math, while their Latino counterparts left high school having completed only geometry. This cross-ethnic disparity reflects overarching trends in Asian achievement (Hao and Bonstead-Bruns 1998), bolstered not only by patterns of immigrant selectivity (Feliciano 2005) but also by community-based academic support for Asian immigrant students' achievements (Bankston and Zhou 2002; Zhou and Kim 2006). We found no discernible differences, however, in course grades, both overall and in math and social science.

We argue that social science coursework in particular has the potential to socialize students for political engagement, independently of the effects of stratification in schools. Exploring this possibility requires, however, that we take into account educational stratification—between and within schools—when estimating social science course experiences. Although in our current political climate we tend to focus on the school as preparing youth for the labor market (Farkas 1996), ultimately, we argue, schools could foster the political engagement of the future generations.

ACCOUNTING FOR BACKGROUND CHARACTERISTICS

Despite the disparities in performance by race and ethnicity, in the bivariate statistics presented in table 4.1 children of immigrants appeared to earn significantly lower grades across subject areas and complete significantly less coursework than did the children of native-born parents. As discussed earlier, however, children of immigrant and native-born parents are often dissimilar on many other factors also known to shape academic achievement and attainment, such as social class, economic background, race, ethnicity, and academic preparation, to name but a few. In considering the achievement of children of immigrants in U.S. schools, it is critical that at minimum we attempt to describe the substantive variations between the immigrant and native-born populations.

To address other factors that also shape achievement, in table 4.2 we present multivariate regression models that predict grades, holding social background constant, and logistic models that predict math and social science course-taking for all students. Here we account not only for the Latino-Asian disparities in performance (see table 4.1) but also for socioeconomic indicators, such as parental education and income and intact family structure. In table 4.2, net of these background characteristics, we see that these models demonstrate an "immigrant advantage": once gender, race-ethnicity, parental education, and other factors are taken into account, children of immigrants took significantly more social science courses and were more likely to complete college preparatory math and social science coursework by the end of high school than children of native-born parents.

The negative association, however, between language minority status and students' grades brings up a critical issue. In U.S. schools, students are not sorted for educational programs based on race, ethnicity, or immigrant status, but rather on the basis of language proficiency. However, language proficiency assessment is not without controversy: it is well understood that identification as an English learner (EL) or as limited English proficient (LEP) varies markedly from state to state, district to district, and often school to school (Mahoney and MacSwan 2005; Ragan and Lesaux 2006), not only with respect to who is identified as in need of linguistic support services, but also with respect to how long students are kept in ESL programs based on their academic achievement (Linquanti 2001; Olsen 2010). ESL program exit criteria require that students demonstrate grade-level achievement, thus unintentionally favoring the exit of Asian immigrant students over other language minority immigrant students who may not demonstrate equally high levels of academic achievement. In the following section, we explore patterns of academic preparation and stratification in U.S. high schools based on linguistic identification.

LANGUAGE AND STRATIFICATION IN U.S. HIGH SCHOOLS

The acquisition of English has always been central to the education of language minority immigrant youth (Tyack 1974). In their explorations of the academic experiences of children of immigrants, researchers must address language proficiency at minimum, if not a wide range of social and background covariates of linguistic identification (ESL placement) and academic achievement as well. Moreover, careful attention must be paid to who is selected into ESL programs; for example, are ESL students recent immigrants or second-generation immigrants? Have they always been enrolled in U.S. schools or are they only recently enrolled? Without addressing such questions, researchers will find it difficult to disentangle the effects on achievement of these other circumstances in the lives of language minority immigrant youths from the effects of placement in ESL.

Another factor to consider is that schools and educators may handle language minority children of immigrants differently than they do children of native-born parents, who are by and large native English speakers. As we noted earlier, many (although not all) children of immigrants speak a language other than English at home. This scenario triggers special consideration within the U.S. school system in that educational policy, partly in response to legal challenges, has been designed to protect the interests of students who are simultaneously learning English and academic content. Under both Castañeda v. Pickard (1981) and Lau v. Nichols (1974), schools must provide some sort of linguistic support services to those language minority youth whose initial assessment for English-language proficiency shows them to be below age level.[1] At the high school level, it is not only the most recent immigrants who enroll in ESL courses (the most common linguistic support service), but also 1.5- and second-generation students. Enrolled since early elementary school, these students have spent most of their school years in U.S. schools, yet remain in ESL services. Although 1.5- and second-generation students do make up a considerable proportion of the high school ESL population (60 to 70 percent by many estimates), ESL students do not make up the majority of the children of immigrants population. By high

Table 4.2   Multivariate Models of High School Academic Achievement and Attainment: Immigrant Status and Other Background Characteristics, 2004

	College Preparatory					
	Math			Social Science		
	ln (B)	Standard Error	Signifi-cant Dif-ference	ln (B)	Standard Error	Signifi-cant Dif-ference
Children of immigrants	0.250	(0.084)	**	0.461	(0.081)	***
Language minority	−0.184	(0.095)		0.057	(0.102)	
Gender	0.393	(0.047)	***	0.366	(0.048)	***
Race (reference: white, non-Hispanic)						
American Indian	−0.875	(0.219)	***	−0.044	(0.272)	
Asian, Hawaiian, or Pacific Islander	0.526	(0.157)	***	0.207	(0.128)	
Black or African American	−0.031	(0.072)		−0.498	(0.087)	***
Hispanic, race unspecified	−0.269	(0.107)	*	−0.551	(0.132)	***
Hispanic, race specified	−0.407	(0.094)	***	−0.647	(0.115)	***
More than one race	−0.335	(0.113)	**	−0.489	(0.129)	***
Parent education (reference: college graduate)						
Less than high school	−0.901	(0.114)	***	−0.785	(0.147)	***
High school or GED	−0.769	(0.077)	***	−0.816	(0.082)	***
Two-year school—no degree	−0.635	(0.086)	***	−0.503	(0.088)	***
Graduated from two-year school	−0.525	(0.087)	***	−0.694	(0.090)	***
Attended college, no four-year degree	−0.387	(0.088)	***	−0.509	(0.086)	***
Completed MA or equivalent	0.131	(0.107)		0.315	(0.076)	***
PhD, MD: advanced degree	0.269	(0.149)		0.367	(0.097)	***
Income	0.008	(0.001)	***	0.003	(0.000)	***
Number of family resources	0.724	(0.132)	***	1.011	(0.151)	***
Intact family structure	0.138	(0.057)	*	0.134	(0.064)	*
Intercept	0.259			−2.064		
N	10,477			10,505		

Source: Education Longitudinal Study (Ingels et al. 2004).

$*p \leq .05$; $**p \leq .01$; $***p \leq .001$

	Overall GPA			Social Science Credits	
Coefficient	Standard Error	Significant Difference	Coefficient	Standard Error	Significant Difference
0.030	(0.023)		0.093	(0.042)	*
−0.076	(0.028)	**	−0.141	(0.050)	**
0.295	(0.013)	***	0.205	(0.024)	***
−0.264	(0.071)	***	0.008	(0.127)	
0.110	(0.038)	**	−0.116	(0.069)	
−0.466	(0.021)	***	−0.154	(0.038)	***
−0.283	(0.033)	***	−0.322	(0.059)	***
−0.277	(0.028)	***	−0.245	(0.051)	***
−0.242	(0.033)	***	−0.189	(0.060)	**
−0.356	(0.035)	***	−0.349	(0.063)	***
−0.279	(0.022)	***	−0.203	(0.039)	***
−0.235	(0.024)	***	−0.150	(0.043)	***
−0.203	(0.024)	***	−0.181	(0.043)	***
−0.182	(0.024)	***	−0.186	(0.043)	***
0.135	(0.024)	***	−0.032	(0.044)	
0.150	(0.031)	***	−0.033	(0.056)	
0.001	(0.000)	***	0.001	(0.000)	***
0.164	(0.043)	***	0.248	(0.074)	***
0.180	(0.017)	***	0.071	(0.030)	*
2.509	(0.038)	***	3.528	(0.067)	***
10,497			10,458		

school, most language minority immigrant youth have become English-proficient, if not English-dominant, no longer require linguistic support services, and have exited ESL programs.

Along with English proficiency, other factors may influence not only the likelihood of immigrant students being placed in ESL coursework but their academic achievement as well. For example, recently arrived immigrants and those whose families are of lower socioeconomic status are more likely to require additional school services and to be placed in ESL courses. Prior empirical work documents that not only recent immigrants but also other, more English-proficient and later-generation students are placed in ESL courses (Faltis and Wolfe 1999; Freeman, Freeman, and Mercuri 2002; Hamann 2008; Olsen 1997). Using the ELS data set, we and our colleague Lindsey Wilkinson investigated the effect of ESL course placement on preparation for college among language minority youth (Callahan et al. 2010). Our analysis drew from an ELS national sample of schools and students to provide an overview of language minority student placement in ESL coursework, which included direct, language-based instruction as well as sheltered and SDAIE (specially designed academic instruction in English) content area coursework. The analysis is based on propensity score matching (PSM), which simultaneously considers many of the factors that predict the likelihood of a student being placed in ESL. Students were matched as closely as possible on an array of measures associated with their chances of being placed in ESL so that the academic outcomes of similar students could be compared.

The findings suggest that among a minority of students—those students who best fit the profile of English learners (ELs), notably, recently arrived immigrants, students from low-income families, and students with relatively low English proficiency—ESL placement has a limited benefit. The majority of students placed in ESL, however, do not fit this profile, and ESL may have a broader negative impact on them. These findings are based on an analysis of outcomes that measured the effects of ESL enrollment by the level of the propensity score stratum, with students divided into high, moderate, and low strata. The majority of ESL students fell into the moderate stratum; only a minority of high-stratum students closely matched the profile of English learners. Relatively few students in the lowest stratum actually experienced ESL placement. Summaries of the results from this analysis are shown in figures 4.1, 4.2, and 4.3, where all within-stratum differences by ESL placement are significant unless otherwise noted.

Figure 4.1 shows the predicted probability, by ESL placement, of completion of college preparatory coursework by the end of high school. Specifically, it shows the probability that students will have completed algebra II or higher (and at least two other math classes), three science credits (including biology), and honors social studies. We chose these academic coursework indicators because they represent preparation for college (Adelman 2006). Pre-

Figure 4.1.   Language Minority Students Completing College Preparatory
Coursework by End of High School, by Likelihood of ESL
Placement, 2004

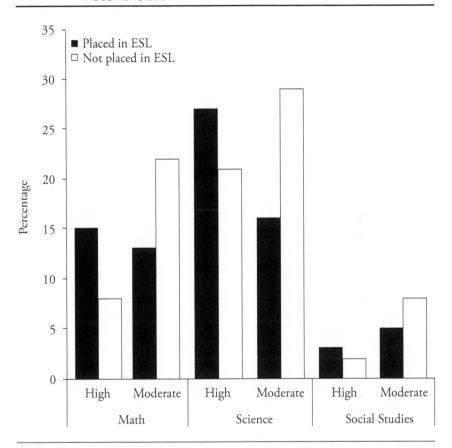

Source: Authors' calculation of data from the Education Longitudinal Study, 2002–2006 (Ingels et al. 2007).

dicted probabilities are shown separately for students who were and were not placed in ESL by whether they were in the high or moderate propensity stratum. For each type of academic course, the students in the moderate stratum—those whose profile was less aligned with that of an expected English learner compared to high-stratum students—had more negative outcomes if they had been placed in ESL. It is possible that ESL course placement indicates that these students were experiencing some type of academic marginalization. In contrast, students in the high stratum appeared to reap benefits

Figure 4.2.   Language Minority Students' Predicted Senior Year Math Test Score, by Likelihood of ESL Placement, 2004

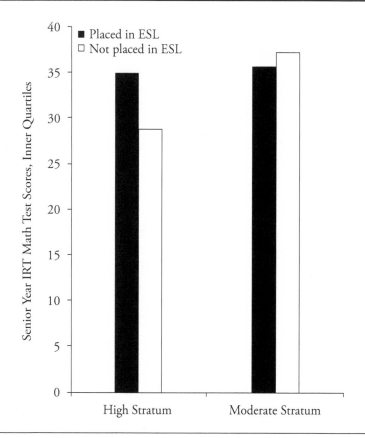

Source: Authors' calculation of data from the Education Longitudinal Study, 2002–2006 (Ingels et al. 2007).

from ESL placement in their math coursework. Figure 4.1 suggests that the ESL students in the high stratum also completed more college preparatory science and social studies, although these differences are not statistically significant.

Figures 4.2 and 4.3 show students' predicted senior year math achievement test scores and cumulative GPA at the end of high school by their likelihood (high/moderate) of placement in ESL. As with coursework, we see a pattern whereby students in the high stratum appeared to benefit academically from ESL placement and those in the moderate stratum did not. It is

Figure 4.3. Language Minority Students' Predicted Cumulative Grade Point Average, by Likelihood of ESL Placement, 2004

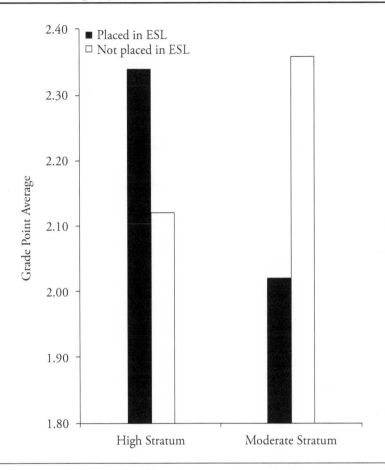

Source: Authors' calculation of data from the Education Longitudinal Study, 2002–2006 (Ingels et al. 2007).

important to underscore that these estimates take into account students' English proficiency, academic performance, and course placement in the early years of high school to try to estimate as accurately as possible the impact of ESL placement during their high school years, as opposed to a cumulative effect that may have begun earlier than high school. Figure 4.2 shows that high-stratum students who were placed in ESL finished high school, on average, with math test scores about six points higher (a little over one-third of a standard deviation) than the scores of similar students who were not placed in ESL. Because students were matched on their freshman and sopho-more year academic performance, these differences are net of any disparities there might have been between them when they entered high school. In con-trast, moderate-stratum students appeared to suffer academically if they were placed in ESL. Figure 4.2 shows slightly lower test scores for the ESL stu-dents, and figure 4.3 shows a gap in GPA of almost one-half of a letter grade disadvantaging moderate-stratum students placed in ESL. In figure 4.3, the apparent gap advantaging ESL students in the high stratum over those not in ESL is not statistically significant.

Together our findings suggest that most adolescent language minority stu-dents do not benefit, and may even be marginalized by, the very ESL pro-grams intended to facilitate their English-language learning. For children of immigrants who are language minority but who are not recently arrived, not poor, and not relatively lacking in English proficiency (those disproportion-ately in our moderate stratum), the presence of a language other than English in the home may serve to marginalize or stratify learning opportunities at school. This is not to say that the use of the native language is itself a threat to these students' achievement, but rather that schools' interpretation of lan-guage minority status and identification of these students with the EL label may limit their academic opportunities.

For recently arrived children of immigrants, especially those who are from poor families and whose English proficiency is low, the main benefit of ESL placement appears to be in the area of mathematics. Considering that aca-demic success in math is highly predictive of college matriculation and post-secondary success (Adelman 2006; Arbona and Nora 2007; Riegle-Crumb 2010), such linguistic support services may be important for the long-term educational and economic success of recently arrived immigrant students.

Conclusions

In sum, we argue that the academic outcomes of children of immigrants, though fairly positive, are still affected by disparities in exposure and oppor-tunity. Importantly, these disparities are related in part to a language issue: identification for and placement in linguistic support services. Our analyses suggest that, inadvertently or not, schools' use of language to structure op-portunity has a disproportionate impact on the educational experiences of children of immigrants, especially in the areas related to college preparation. That schools stratify educational access to higher education is not necessarily new (Gamoran 1992; Lucas 1999; Oakes 1985; Warikoo and Carter 2009); however, the role of language in that process is less well understood. It ap-pears that how schools address and operationalize language assessment and support services is related to students' preparation for postsecondary educa-tion and in this way indirectly shapes their political development.

Not only does placement in ESL coursework constrain achievement among language minority children of immigrants, as we demonstrate here, but it also limits their overall curricular exposure. For the relatively English-proficient immigrant youth, time in their schedules dedicated to ESL coursework is time not spent in math, science, or social science coursework. The student placed in ESL is less free to take band, theater, and the other electives associated with enhanced school belonging, academic achievement, and future civic engagement.

There is a second way in which high schools may shape political participation and contribute more directly to students' civic preparation: social science course-taking. As a content area, social science is unique in its accessibility to all, and unlike math, it is not organized sequentially. Because certain social science courses, most notably U.S. history and state history, are often state-mandated, they are generally taken by almost all students. Beyond these basic courses, there is substantial heterogeneity in social science course-taking patterns, as we shall see. Social science coursework may be uniquely accessible to children of immigrants—buffered as it is from the traditional stratification that limits access to math, science, and honors courses—and may also speak to their experiences as they navigate between the world of school and the world of home and parents. In the next chapter, we will see how children of immigrants, tasked with bridging two cultures, if not two worlds, respond to social science curriculum as they make their way through the U.S. high school system.

CHAPTER 5

Social Science Preparation and the Adolescent Children of Immigrants

We turn our attention now to the second way in which schools prepare students for political participation: the social science courses designed to develop civic knowledge and skills. Since its inception, the U.S. high school has evolved to guide youth toward professional and civic participation in adult society, and all high schools today simultaneously prepare youth for college, for the workforce, and for civic life by setting minimum graduation requirements for all students and college eligibility requirements for others. In fact, with the expansion in secondary school enrollment during the last century, high school course-taking now contributes significantly to social stratification among American youth. But the social science curriculum also has the potential to develop engaged, civic-minded young adults who are focused on their role in the larger community (Ravitch 2010). The quality and quantity of social science coursework completed during high school plays a major role in the opportunities that become available during young adulthood, whether through college enrollment (Adelman 2004) or direct entry into the labor market.

Social Science: Civic Development Through Schooling

As schools prepare youth to participate in the economic sector as well as in civic society (Cremin 1951; Goodlad 1984; Hart et al. 2007), they play a central role in the civic development of children of immigrants. Both first- and second-generation youth come from homes in which the parents are relatively new participants in the U.S. political system. As communities and institutions, schools are the first, if not the primary, source of information regarding civic engagement, education, and development in the adopted homeland. This may be especially salient in immigrant families where the parents are preparing for their own naturalization and citizenship while their children are being socialized in the discourse of the social science classroom.[1] The parallels between immigrant parents' and their children's political development may provide opportunities for deeper discussion and exploration of a common theme in the home.

SOCIAL SCIENCE EDUCATION

The field of social science education has evolved considerably since its inception during the social welfare movement of the 1850s (Saxe 1992). By the turn of the twentieth century, scholars were seeking to expand the field by taking new theories from the emerging social sciences (for example, sociology, psychology, and political science) and applying them to patterns of political and civic activity. A century and a half later, K-12 social science education has expanded to include the development of participatory citizens (Levstik and Barton 2001; Nelson 2001; Parker 2001a). During adolescence, social science coursework is associated with the development of civic knowledge (Gamoran 1987); in turn, civic knowledge provides the foundation for future political participation (Atherton 2000; Chaffee 2000; Dudley and Gitelson 2002). Social science instruction also builds both civic knowledge and trust in government (Torney-Purta, Richardson, and Barber 2004), which are necessary for future political participation.

In serving its dual purpose—preparing students for higher education (Adelman 2004) as well as for civic engagement in young adulthood (Atherton 2000; Chaffee 2000; Niemi and Junn 1998)—high school social science coursework covers not only civics but also world and U.S. history, geography, and electives such as international relations, sociology, psychology, and political science (Jenness 1990; Thornton 1994). The sequential order of course-taking may vary across schools, but general history and government tend to dominate the high school curriculum and are taken by most high school graduates (Fallace 2008; Ross 1997). Most general history courses (U.S., world, and state) fulfill high school graduation requirements, while additional social science course-taking (honors classes, for instance, or electives such as political science) contributes to college preparation. In his analysis, Adam Gamoran (1987) found little variation in the amount of social science coursework completed net of students' track placement (college preparatory versus general education), but he did find a significant association between the number of social science credits and students' civic knowledge, a measure of social science preparation. Importantly, this association between civics course-taking and knowledge held even after both track placement and math achievement, as measured by test scores, were held constant.

CIVIC PREPARATION: CURRICULAR ACCESS

The vulnerability of today's high school to political tensions surrounding the social science curriculum is only one threat to the civic goals of education; equally important is the variation in the quality of the social science coursework that students encounter. Social science offerings vary in both quality and quantity across school types (Nation's Report Card 2010), and immigrant students, who typically attend lower-quality schools, are more likely to receive limited and weak social science instruction. The quality of courses varies not only across types and levels of schools but also within schools, as might be expected in our increasingly stratified school system (Garet and DeLany 1988). Jean Anyon (1988) demonstrates that students are taught differently depending on the level of the course, a critical point to keep in mind with respect to students' accumulation of social science credits. Since high school requirements for history and government credits are fairly standard for all students, there is little variation in the accumulation of these credits; rather, students who accumulate more than the basic requirements tend to do so through course-taking in electives. Further differentiation in the accumulation of credits occurs when students take honors-level or AP courses, such as AP U.S. history. To some extent, these sources of variation covary with students' other courses. For example, college-bound students are likely to take more advanced math along with their honors coursework (Riegle-Crumb 2006). Addressing early high school course placement and achievement allows the researcher to account for students' academic status and standing.

Differences in social science preparation emerge relatively early in the academic pipeline. In an analysis of students' civic knowledge and preparation for citizenship using data from the IEA Civic Education Study, Judith Torney-Purta, Carolyn Barber, and Britt Wilkenfeld (2006) report disparities in civic knowledge by immigrant status among fourteen-year-olds. The authors find that non-immigrant, non-Hispanic fourteen-year-olds in the United States demonstrate greater civic knowledge, understanding of democracy, and political communication skills than their immigrant and Hispanic peers. Similar patterns arise when comparing Hispanic students' scores to white students' on the National Assessment of Education Progress (NAEP) test of civic knowledge in grades eight and twelve (Nation's Report Card 2010): the gap has decreased, but it remains statistically significant. Grade-level patterns in the gap in civic knowledge are consistent with the emergence of other achievement gaps (in math, for instance) and call into question the extent to which the observed civic knowledge gap is simply a function of school stratification, which is in turn related to educational attainment over the life course. Although the root source of the civic knowledge gap remains unclear, these findings suggest that children of immigrants exit high school with lower levels of civic knowledge, which in turn may be attributable to their social science course-taking.

The quantity and type of social science coursework in which students enroll contribute not only to their preparation for higher education (Adelman 2004; Nation's Report Card 2010) but also to their civic participation in young adulthood (Atherton 2000; Callahan et al. 2008; Niemi and Junn 1998). Social science electives (such as geography, political science, international relations, and sociology or psychology) may offer access to a wider range of curricular content in the social sciences. Our analyses of voting behavior in chapter 6 account for both students' overall academic status as it is related to college preparation and their social science–specific preparation.

IMMIGRANT STUDENTS' SOCIAL SCIENCE COURSE-TAKING

Social science coursework is relevant to many aspects of the immigrant experience. In high school, social science coursework is designed to encourage students' knowledge of and ability to participate in civic society as young adults (Parker 2005; Sherrod et al. 2002). For children of immigrants, courses that feature the history of the United States and its political system or comparative analyses of the United States and other cultures may provide important knowledge as well as an opportunity to share their own experiences in the classroom setting. The degree to which adolescent children of immigrants enroll in social science coursework may vary, however, depending on the structure of the course offerings.

A student's social science experience may depend not only on individual characteristics but also on characteristics of the school the student attends. Prior research exploring segmented assimilation theory (Bankston and Zhou 2002; Portes and Zhou 1993; Rumbaut and Portes 2001; Zhou 1997b) suggests that the proportion of co-ethnics or co-immigrants in the community influences young adults' professional and social integration. Although it is not a centerpiece to our argument, we do take the proportion of immigrant youth at a school into account when predicting social science course-taking.

High school social science course-taking may provide the primary source of civic engagement for the children of immigrants. As we have already explored college preparatory course-taking by linguistic status among children of immigrants, we turn our attention now to cumulative social science preparation. In table 5.1, we show social science course-taking patterns for both immigrant and third-plus-generation students using the Add Health data set. These patterns suggest that children of immigrants' social science preparation differs significantly from that of their third-plus-generation counterparts. Although adolescent children of immigrants take significantly more courses in general history, they also take fewer political science, elective, and advanced social science courses, as reflected in their significantly lower levels of overall course-taking. Although we cannot definitively determine the motivations behind these trends, we do note that general history coursework often meets local high school graduation requirements. In contrast, political science and advanced social science coursework are often college preparatory courses that prepare a student to enter higher education. This distinction reflects a ten-

Table 5.1   Mean Social Science Credits by Generational Status, 1994–2000

	Children of Immigrants (N = 2,445)	Children of Native-Born (N = 9,128)	Significant Difference
Course-taking			
General history	1.929	1.748	***
Political science	0.956	1.024	***
Geography	0.260	0.437	***
Sociology or psychology	0.282	0.375	***
Non-Western history	0.168	0.199	*
Other history	0.546	0.592	*
Achievement			
Social science GPA	2.473	2.449	
Social science credits	3.364	3.490	***

Source: Add Health (Bearman et al. 1997) and AHAA (Muller et al. 2007).
$*p \le .05; ***p \le .001$

dency to prepare language minority immigrant students for high school graduation but not much else (Callahan and Gándara 2004). This pattern in social science course-taking also bolsters our finding that although students' social science grades do not vary significantly by immigrant status, there is significant variation in their overall social science preparation, as measured in credits completed.

These qualitative and quantitative differences in social science preparation suggest that adolescent children of immigrants' social science preparation lags behind that of their third-plus-generation peers in terms of credits completed, especially in elective and advanced courses. Government and other such coursework prepares students directly for both higher education and civic engagement in adulthood (Atherton 2000; Chaffee 2000; Niemi and Junn 1998), preparation that children of immigrants are less likely to receive in the home. In addition, college readiness is a key factor in the pathway to political engagement.

Immigrant Youths' Position and Teachers' Practices

Patterns in social science course-taking may be particularly relevant for immigrant youth. The goal of the social science curriculum is to produce enlightened political engagement (Parker 2001b), and the classroom can often maximize the ability of adolescent children of immigrants to put civics lessons into practice (Sherrod et al. 2002). To better understand the nuances of the social science experiences of children of immigrants, we designed a supplemental qualitative study (see appendix for greater detail). We limited the complexity of our story by focusing on Latino children of immigrants for two reasons: the 2010 decennial census revealed that there has been rapid growth in the proportion of Latinos in the school-age population, and Asian children of immigrants face many confounding issues in U.S. schools. This decision was buoyed by the rich recent literature on Latinos' political involvement cited earlier as well as by the focus on Latinos in current immigration debates.

More specifically, we explored through interviews (see chapter 1 and the appendix for details) those aspects of the social science classroom that may shape students' pathways to civic engagement. In this series of open-ended interviews with nationally board-certified high school social science teachers and Latino immigrant young adults in five key immigrant-receiving communities, we set out to better understand teachers' and students' perspectives on what actually happens in advanced high school social science courses—such as AP and honors U.S. history, American government, and world studies—that might facilitate the political engagement of this growing population of new citizens at the turn of a new century. We chose exemplary social science teachers who emphasized skills and strategies that would resonate particularly well among immigrant youth. As the Latino population continues to grow at an unprecedented rate (Passel and Cohn 2008; U.S. Census Bureau 2006), ensuring the "enlightened political engagement" (Parker 2001b) of its youth will only strengthen our democracy in the future.

PEDAGOGY AND PERSPECTIVES

Although the social science curriculum itself is undoubtedly central to learning, several studies exploring the social science classroom highlight the importance of teachers' pedagogical practices in the development of political engagement among youth. For example, Joseph Kahne, Bernadette Chi, and Ellen Middaugh (2006) argue that teachers' practices shape political engagement later in life. Interactive, inquiry-based pedagogies can create opportunities for students to construct knowledge rather than reproduce it (Newmann, Marks, and Gamoran 1996). In addition, such practices enable students to practice important civic skills, such as construction of an argument, deliberation, and negotiation.

The ability to understand the position of another individual lies at the core of civic life, and social science teachers are tasked with developing this ability in the voters of tomorrow. In an overview of the pedagogical research, Geert ten Dam and Monique Volman (2004) suggest that even though teachers can create environments where multiple perspectives are recognized and defended, ultimately students must develop these skills within themselves. The work of Anand Marri (2005) shows how high school social science teachers who are effective at transmitting a multicultural democratic education actively engage their students in developing critical thinking skills. These teachers require that students engage with the information at hand, effectively communicate their position to others, and negotiate multiple perspectives. Such open, safe environments where students can engage in debate and discussion have been shown to contribute to schools' ability to foster civic engagement (Torney-Purta 2002). Through this link between pedagogy and context we explore immigrant young adults' political and civic coming of age. We begin by sharing composite portraits of our participants, both the teachers and the Latino immigrant young adults.

High School Social Science Teachers   The desire to foster enlightened political engagement (Parker 2001b) in the next generation is the central goal of high school social science curriculum in the United States (Atherton 2000), and our participants' interviews reflected a perspective consistent with this purpose. Although we did not ask the teachers to name the specific texts and resources they used, they consistently reported covering similar content and using many of the same strategies in their classrooms, more than likely owing to the shared descriptions of advanced social science courses and the focus of much of the coursework on the common AP exams (Rothschild 1999). Overall, the teacher participants provided a comprehensive overview of their perceptions of their role, the role of the curriculum and instruction, and their expectations of their students in terms of civic engagement.

Latino Immigrant Young Adults   The Latino immigrant young adult participants exhibited noteworthy levels of civic engagement and dedication to the community. Each of the Latino young adults described considerable civic participation on their college campus, and many had taken on leadership roles and integrated themselves into the surrounding community as well. Nearly all participated in some form of political outreach in their community during the 2008 presidential election: organizing voter registration drives, holding debates, volunteering on campaigns, spearheading fund-raisers, and developing Facebook forums. Besides holding leadership positions, many of them mentored other undergraduates and middle and high school students; led community service projects; and volunteered in the campus and city health care clinics, providing health education services. Their employment also leaned toward civic-minded pursuits: one of our participants was an advocate in the student disabilities office, another interned on a Senate campaign, and yet another worked as a health sexuality peer educator.

Perceptions of the Social Science Context: Bridging Worlds

As our analysis of the interview data progressed, three interrelated themes emerged: bridging worlds, multiple perspectives, and critical thinking.

BRIDGING WORLDS

Our data suggest that for the most part children of immigrants and their third-plus-generation peers interact with the social science curriculum in similar ways; however, both teachers and young adults pointed out that immigrants' bridging experiences (Cooper et al. 2002) make some aspects of the social science curriculum particularly salient to them. Teachers remarked that children of immigrants' ability to perceive alternative viewpoints facilitated their understanding of civics lessons. Likewise, the comments of immigrant young adults suggested that they were aware of their teachers' perspective on their contributions to the classroom from their lived experiences.

MULTIPLE PERSPECTIVES

By definition, children of immigrants come to the high school social science classroom having already begun to negotiate their position between two worlds—the home and the school. Our findings suggest that social science teachers' emphasis on multiple perspectives resonates with the lived experiences of children of immigrants. This idea was confirmed by Isabel, a twenty-year-old student in San Diego of Mexican origin: "I think it was a very important stepping-stone for us . . . to develop sensitivity towards people. And I think with the two different cultures, we were already made sensitive since birth . . . but we developed . . . a lot more sensitivity in that class. It helped us a lot." Like Isabel, many of our participants actively engaged with their social science teachers' civic discourse, feeling a personal connection not only to the teachers but to the social science content being taught.

Professionally focused on shaping the civic engagement of the next generation, these social science teachers were acutely aware that their immigrant students might identify with the curriculum and the content in a way that children of native-born parents might not. Teachers viewed children of immigrants' exposure to other political systems as a motivator to engage in the political sphere in their adopted U.S. system. Mr. Tomasi, a world history teacher from San Diego, specifically observed a "sense of urgency" among the families of his immigrant students; he noted that they were "trying to better [their] situation—and politically, that means voting." Likewise, Mr. Jones, the U.S. history teacher in Florida, noted that immigrants "come here, they see opportunity, they see freedom . . . many of the things they fled from, and they are eager to participate. But in order to participate, they have got to become informed and knowledgeable about the system." The young adults themselves, though not always able to articulate why, recognized that they approached the social studies forum in high school with a perspective different from that of their peers born to U.S.-born parents. Anthony, a twenty-four-year-old of Mexican origin living in Texas, said: "I knew I was kind of, I don't want to say disadvantaged, but I would say the stories around me were just one-sided . . . I knew where I was. There are people with different opinions, different races and creeds and backgrounds, that can have a different opinion." Like their teachers—and like Anthony—the Latino immigrant youth we interviewed recognized that they had been marginalized socially and politically and saw the social science curriculum as speaking directly to their experiences.

In fact, teachers capitalized on their students' dual points of reference and position outside mainstream U.S. society, highlighting their experiences as the voice of "the other." Teachers used the experiences of their children of immigrant students to link the social science curriculum to all students' lives (consistent with the discussion of the construction of knowledge in Newmann, Marks, and Gamoran 1996). As the Latino immigrant young adults were bridging two worlds in high school, they were constructing—rather than reproducing—knowledge by drawing on their life experiences to develop their civic understanding.

In addition, their experiences and their voices became a part of the valued content of the course. Civil rights was a popular topic, and teachers encouraged students to relate the course content to their own lives. Ms. McDougal, a U.S. and world history teacher in Chicago, gave an example from her classroom:

> Right now we're talking about Jim Crow, and the grandfather clauses, and the polling taxes, and the literacy tests. . . . What does it mean to not be able to understand the ballot? . . . When I'm with my mom's group, it's "You're an American. You should learn to speak English. Our documents should not be published in any other language but English." I say this to my kids: "That is what my mother's generation thinks, the World War II generation." [I ask,] "How do you respond to that? Okay. Why? Let's talk about that. Well, what languages should it be available in?" "Well, Spanish." "Is that the only one?" "Well, we're the dominant minority." "So you're going to lock out the other minorities? How about before you were the dominant minority?" "Oh." "Well, what other languages are important?" "Well, because we are in a school with Polish-speaking kids, well, we can have Polish." "Okay. Is that it?" "Well, I don't think that we should have whatever languages they speak in the Middle East." "Well, why not?" "Because they're all terrorists." Okay. Here we go

again. We're going to have to have that conversation. But it's uncovering what they think.

Here Ms. McDougal challenged her students, themselves children of immigrants, to consider the stereotyped perceptions they might hold of others. Although they had been on the receiving end of discriminatory behavior, they were also adolescents—quick to pass judgment on another group. Ms. McDougal's consistency in her interrogation of students' meaning-making here reflected her determination to prepare these immigrant youth for active engagement in the civic discourse of their communities, now and in adulthood. Children of immigrants, by definition, constantly take into account how "the other" perceives the world. A central premise of the social science curriculum is that learning to recognize others' (multiple) perspectives is necessary in order to persuade, engage, and lead.

In fact, leadership emerged as a central theme among the immigrant young adult participants. In discussing her role engaging other college students in the presidential debates, Amanda, a twenty-one-year-old Latina of Mexican origin living in Texas, highlighted her ability to employ the discourse of her peers:

I've been . . . keeping up with politics since middle school. . . . I am one of those crazy outliers. I just draw on past knowledge. Since I'm in a younger category, with people who are just now being able to vote . . . I'll try to keep it light, keep references to *SNL* or stuff like that that everybody knows about. So I'll be like, look at Palin on *SNL,* or, you know, Tina Fey on *SNL,* and draw that into the conversation and then try to cut deeper from there.

Having recognized her strong attraction to politics from an early age, Amanda had expanded her civic engagement beyond voting, which she was always inclined to do, to encouraging her peers to vote. She saw her role as that of an actor working to raise awareness among her peers. Amanda had responded to the challenges posed in her social science coursework by becoming a leader among her peers, and from that position she could initiate and negotiate civic discourse and political participation.

CRITICAL THINKING SKILLS

If one key to becoming politically engaged in young adulthood is learning to recognize and utilize others' perspectives, another is the art of persuasion. Using social science content as a springboard to develop and defend an argument, our target teachers guided their students in taking a position and defending it with evidence, a hallmark of authentic intellectual work (Newmann et al. 1996). The Latino young adults repeatedly remarked on their teachers' insistence that they be able to defend a position different from their own. Both teachers and immigrant youth spoke of the importance of argumentation, the ability to seek out, identify, and employ evidence to support one's position. Teachers referred directly and indirectly to the multilayered argumentation process used in debates and role-plays, which requires the defense of a perspective. In fact, the content of the activity was secondary to the thought process being developed. Mr. Gordon, who taught Latin American studies in Chicago, explained:

> My goal is to develop critical thinking through the manipulation of evidence—through the manipulation of information. . . . It's really a skills-oriented class. So in any given year I ask them, "What topics do you want to look at?" We're going to go over a set of skills. We are going to work on skill sets. The content is almost irrelevant.

Teachers' emphasis on critical thinking skills—argumentation, evaluation of evidence, articulation of one's perspective—drove all of the participants' reflections about the formative aspects of high school social science coursework. Teachers reported engaging students in activities that forced them to question, and later to defend, competing positions, and as noted earlier, and students reported being aware of their teacher's insistence on the importance of these skills.

Argumentation   Our participants valued the classroom activities that required students to question assumptions, evaluate evidence, and draw from historical and current primary sources of evidence. Teachers reflected on the oral debates and role-plays they initiated, as well as other argumentation activities that encompassed reading and writing designed to motivate students to critically evaluate information. Mr. Tomasi, a world history teacher in San Diego, said:

> Well, I think there are things that we do in our curriculum . . . where you challenge, [you] don't accept the status quo just because someone's saying it, that's where you go back to the source. *Who's* saying it? *Why* are they saying it? *What's* the endgame? *What* are the objectives? Look at it that way. Try to be more objective . . . dispassionate. [Find out] more of the story and don't get caught up in the emotions. Try to understand what's being said, for what purpose. . . . I think the government class talks a lot about these issues, whether it's corruption or certain cases.

A Chicago civics and government teacher, Ms. Jewel, described one of her classroom activities:

In my law class they have to find a current events article that has to do with law. And they have to identify any bias in the article, in the headline, in the article. You know, I'm trying to get them to read, be thinking readers. And so that gives us an opportunity to talk about the media and the media's influence on us as consumers of the media.

Here we can see teachers' motivation to engage their students in the civic discourse of the outside world. These teachers recognized that as children of immigrants, some of their students had the potential to become leaders in their communities, and they pushed these students all the more passionately to be discerning consumers of information.

Beyond writing a persuasive essay, as they might have done in their English or other humanities classes, our young adult participants recalled the preparation required of them to debate key topics with and in front of their peers. Classroom discussions provide a forum in which one can learn to defend a position (Flynn 2009; Newstreet 2008; Parker 2010), a particularly relevant skill for immigrant young adults. Children of immigrants must learn to participate in a political system that is new to both them and their parents, and several students recounted, with mock frustration, their teachers' hard-nosed tactics in teaching them how to participate. Ultimately, however, they praised the outcome. For instance, Fernando, a twenty-one-year-old in Texas of Guatemalan and Argentinean origin, had this to say:

[My government teacher] was really good at wanting you to say what you really feel about a subject. And so you sort of get angry because he's baiting you into these things. You lay out your opinion, and then he will ask you, "Why do you think that?" And that question . . . puts you on edge . . . you have to go back and rethink everything to double-check that, yes, this is really what I think.

Fernando's teacher used strong-arm tactics to challenge his students and prepare them for the often-vicious discourse of public debates. Our immigrant young adult participants frequently reflected on their teachers' insistence that they fortify their arguments in preparation to take on a leadership role in their communities. Amanda in Texas, for example, said that her teacher "would be just like, 'No, if you have a position, you better damn well be able to back it up, or else I am not going to listen to you, and I'm not going to let anyone else listen to you [either].'"

These teachers recognized that their students, as relatively well-educated children of immigrants, would be in the position to broker their two worlds. Schooled in the discourse of the home and in that of the greater civic sphere, these children of immigrants, as young adults, would be poised to become leaders not only within their coethnic communities but also among their peers.

These young adults' use of argumentation and other civic discourse skills was not limited to the outside world by any means. In fact, many brought these newly developed skills and strategies to political discussions with their families. Many of the young adults articulated an awareness of their unique position not only as children of immigrants in a classroom context dominated by children of native-born parents but also as the first in their family or community to attend college. Sam, a twenty-one-year-old living in Texas and originally from Mexico, observed that

> every once in a while my mom will say something about a certain politician, and I won't refute her opinions or her stances on a political sense, but . . . I've taken a lot of classes that force you to think critically and ask these kinds of questions. So, when I ask my mom, "What about this or what about that?" And seeing what she says and what she thinks and what she feels, I feel like a lot of her opinions . . . most of it comes from what the news sources say. And like a lot of her friends that she talks with about a lot of these things, they have the same news sources. . . . I just want—I guess from my own point of view, [that] she's thought about these things in a different sense, more critically.

This young adult's desire to maintain a respectful stance in his home, while also prompting family members to think critically about information sources and potential biases, suggests a sensitivity to others' perspectives and positions. Ultimately, argumentation strategies are useful in teaching that the student's voice is important and needs to be respected, but is best heard when supported with fact.

Debates   Another popular activity designed to shape students' ability to adopt and defend opposing viewpoints is the classroom debate on a popular social or political topic. Although their classroom debates did not follow formal rules, the teachers were careful to ensure that students could not always select the position they favored. Ms. Martínez, a European and world history teacher in Texas, said:

> Every single time [we debate] I debrief. . . . I always ask the students . . . "How many of you were on the side that you wanted to be on?" And it's roughly half . . . so we talk about, "Well, how did you go about researching for this when you didn't believe it? How did you actually consider arguments?" . . . You have to take . . . almost an entire class period . . . to talk about what those connections are and why that question was important.

Many of the Latino young adults credited the teachers who created the most challenging situations with inspiring them to become engaged in the civic and political life of their communities. In fact, several reported being motivated by particularly difficult experiences learning to debate. Fatima, a twenty-year-old Mexican-origin young adult in San Diego, said that "one . . . very big part of what made me specifically want to get my opinions out was she made us participate in debates. And it was very interesting. . . . I argued for the legalization of prostitution, and my views are not in accordance with that. But I wanted a challenge." Ms. McDougal, the Chicago history teacher, noted that debates provide "such a wonderful growing experience and knowledge experience for them to get up on stage, conduct these debates, have to defend their positions, let their colleagues listen to them, and then have the groups make informed decisions."

The public nature of debates makes it important to know how to evaluate evidence, articulate a position, and orally defend an argument. Debates allowed the children of immigrants in our study to practice adult political discourse and prepared them for future political engagement—a core goal of the social science curriculum.

Role-Plays The social science teachers also capitalized on students' experiences through role-plays and debates to prompt them to reflect on current political issues. Ms. Martínez used role-play to explore with her students the tenuous nature of our civil liberties and to practice incorporating the perspective of another person.

> Imagine that you're a Jew living in Germany and you never know when they're going to revoke your citizenship . . . you live in fear every day. Here you are contributing what you can to society and you never know; they can take it away. And so we talk about that with the new immigrants coming in as well. And . . . it connects it, not because they read it, but because they actually experienced those feelings even if it was only for two weeks. You know, they experienced those feelings. They felt that they knew what that was like. . . . They become so invested in their roles.

Like Ms. McDougal, Ms. Martínez also guided her students to connect issues in the social science curriculum with current policy issues relevant to immigrants. The relationship between today's aggressively anti-immigrant discourse and Nazi xenophobia was not lost on her students, nor on other children of immigrants. In fact, learning to connect these experiences may actually spur political participation among the growing population of children of immigrants (Pantoja, Ramirez, and Segura 2001; Ramakrishnan and Espenshade 2001). Ms. Martínez and the other teacher participants encouraged all their students to link curricular content to their lived experiences; this was an especially relevant exercise for adolescent children of immigrants trying to link their parents' experiences to the experiences of past generations.

Teachers also used role-plays to develop in their students a sense of the agency of individual actors in history and empathy for them (Seixas 1993). This was yet another aspect of the social science curriculum that was particularly salient to the lived experiences of children of immigrants—in this case, their experience in adopting and negotiating multiple perspectives. This lived experience complemented a curricular focus on the critical thinking skills necessary to manage different viewpoints. Where academic expectations are high, developing these attributes may lead to the political engagement of young adult leaders.

Immigrants' Academic Experiences: Background, Language, and Academic Placement

Having explored children of immigrants' social science experiences in depth, we move on to explore their overall high school achievement. The racial-ethnic achievement gap in American society is well documented in the research literature, which dates back to the turn of the century (Fuller and Hannum 2002; Lucas 1999; Warikoo and Carter 2009). Stratification of educational opportunities and outcomes in U.S. schools may play out along racial-ethnic lines (Kao and Thompson 2003) as well as socioeconomic lines (Crosnoe and Huston 2007). Extending the arguments set forth by Jane Junn (1999) and Wendy Cho (1999), we note that the stratification of educational opportunities experienced by youth in the educational system may later influence the relationship between their SES and political participation. Children of immigrants, who are more likely to be both minority language speakers and of lower socioeconomic status, may be especially prone to social and academic marginalization (Olsen 1997). Prior research documents these patterns within the children of immigrants population (Rumbaut and Portes 2001), as well as among children of native-born parents (Lucas and Berends 2007). Disparities in academic preparation based on immigrant status may shape the political participation of the next generation of voters.

In addition, schools must balance the unique educational and linguistic needs of children of immigrants as they integrate these students into the core academic coursework (Deschenes, Cuban, and Tyack 2001; Tyack 2003). Much of the educational literature regarding adolescent children of immigrants in schools focuses on their progress in learning English; we take this into consideration with variables that address both English proficiency (via Picture Vocabulary Test [PVT] scores) and placement in ESL coursework (discussed in greater detail in chapter 4). In a similar vein, students' course-taking and academic preparation in secondary school determine their viability in higher education and in the professional world (Ingels et al. 2002).

Academic preparation occurs within and across a stratified educational system (Gamoran 1987; Stevenson, Schiller, and Schneider 1994); understanding students' academic preparation, immigrant or not, requires taking into account their individual position within the academic hierarchy of the school. For children of immigrants in particular, social science preparation may be associated not only with their immigrant status but also with their language status and prior academic placement.

IMMIGRANT YOUTH: SOCIAL SCIENCE PREPARATION

To explore the association between immigrant status and social science preparation, we first model students' social science performance as measured by their grade point average (GPA) in social science. Our models take into account a range of factors that influence student achievement and enrollment. Table 5.2 shows the coefficients predicting social science grades using data from the National Longitudinal Study of Adolescent Health (Add Health) and the Adolescent Health and Academic Achievement Study (AHAA). These models also take into account the clustering of students in schools, and the final model controls for the percentage of immigrant students in the school. Although it is still possible that our estimated effects are a result of school differences, our multilevel approach reduces the possibility that these differences are unmeasured and driving any individual-level differences that we observe.

Model 1, our baseline model, indicates that there is no significant association between immigrant status and social science grades: children of immigrants earned social science grades similar to those of children of native-born parents. However, immigrant status becomes significant once we take race, ethnicity, and socioeconomic characteristics into account in model 2. For a given level of social background, children of immigrants excelled at school, on average earning about one-eighth of a letter grade higher in social science GPA by the end of high school. The higher social science grades at the end of high school earned by children of immigrants are explained by their academic preparation and their attitudes, suggesting that their social science performance was part of the well-documented overall profile of children of immigrants as relatively high achievers.

We also explore the number of social science credits that students completed as a measure of civic preparation, using the Add Health data (table 5.3). The first model shows that, on average, children of immigrants earned fewer social science credits by the end of high school compared to third-plus-generation students. This difference is explained when their social background characteristics are taken into account, as shown in model 2. The third model introduces the academic factors associated with the accumulation of

Table 5.2   OLS Regression Coefficients from Models Predicting Social Science Grade
Point Average

	Model 1: Baseline		Model 2: Individual Background		Model 3: Language and Academics	
Intercept	2.51	(0.01)***	2.00	(0.07)***	−0.17	(0.09)
Immigrant	0.03	(0.02)	0.13	(0.03)***	0.04	(0.03)
Background characteristics						
Female			0.31	(0.02)***	0.25	(0.01)***
Black			−0.36	(0.02)***	−0.23	(0.02)***
Latino Mexican			−0.19	(0.04)***	−0.01	(0.03)
Latino non-Mexican			−0.24	(0.04)***	−0.12	(0.04)
Asian			0.04	(0.05)	0.03	(0.04)**
Other			−0.26	(0.05)***	−0.16	(0.04)***
Parental education level			0.15	(0.01)***	0.05	(0.00)***
Intact family structure			0.26	(0.02)***	0.12	(0.01)***
Age			−0.02	(0.00)***	−0.01	(0.00)*
Language and academics						
PVT					0.01	(0.00)***
ESL					0.15	(0.05)**
Highest math course taken					0.24	(0.00)***
College aspirations					0.06	(0.01)***
Percentage immigrant in school					−0.15	(0.05)**
N	11,108		10,982		10,460	

Source: Add Health (Bearman et al. 1997) and AHAA (Muller et al. 2007).
Note: Standard errors are shown in parentheses.
*$p \leq .05$; **$p \leq .01$; ***$p \leq .001$

social science credits; however, the coefficient for children of immigrants remains statistically insignificant, suggesting that there is no difference in social
science credit accumulation between children of immigrants and children of
native-born parents. It is important to note that this advantage persists even
when taking into account the between-school variation accounted for in the
negative relationship between high-immigrant-serving schools and social science credit accumulation. Other factors that contribute to social science
credit completion are certainly of interest as well, and in the following chapter we explore several of these factors that may predict the political participation and party identification of youth in our sample.

Table 5.3   OLS Regression Coefficients from Models Predicting Social Science Credits

	Model 1: Baseline		Model 2: Individual Background		Model 3: Language and Academics	
Intercept	3.63	(0.01)***	3.96	(0.10)***	2.58	(0.14)***
Immigrant	−0.12	(0.03)***	−0.01	(0.04)	−0.05	(0.04)
Background characteristics						
Female			0.17	(0.02)***	0.11	(0.02)***
Black			0.05	(0.03)	0.11	(0.03)***
Latino Mexican			−0.20	(0.05)***	−0.06	(0.05)
Latino non-Mexican			0.03	(0.06)	0.14	(0.06)*
Asian			−0.01	(0.06)	−0.04	(0.06)
Other			−0.08	(0.06)	−0.01	(0.06)
Parental education level			0.11	(0.01)***	0.04	(0.01)***
Intact family structure			0.16	(0.02)***	0.05	(0.02)*
Age			−0.06	(0.01)***	−0.05	(0.01)***
Language and academics						
PVT					0.00	(0.00)***
ESL					0.05	(0.08)
Highest math course taken					0.17	(0.01)***
College aspirations					0.07	(0.01)***
Percentage immigrant in school					−0.16	(0.07)*
N	11,122		10,996		10,474	

Source: Add Health (Bearman et al. 1997) and AHAA (Muller et al. 2007).

Note: Standard errors are shown in parentheses.

*p ≤ .05; ***p ≤ .001

Conclusions

Although we initially observed differences in credit accumulation when comparing children of immigrants and children of native-born parents—especially across the different topic areas within the social sciences (table 5.1)—ultimately children of immigrants' social science coursework appeared to follow patterns similar to those of their non-immigrant counterparts. The bivariate differences we observed may lead to variation in the development of civic knowledge, a measure we were unable to explore within the constraints of our data sets. In other words, the academic stratification documented in chapter 4 may explain the variation in course credits and social science grades by immigrant status, but the limitations in our data prevent us from determining whether course-taking and grades are in fact related to civic knowledge. Prior research does link the accumulation of social science credits with the development of civic knowledge (Gamoran 1987), a relationship that, we hypothesize, may be central to preparing the next generation of citizens. Our questions, however, pertain to the association between social science course-taking and performance and our outcome of interest, political participation in young adulthood.

As evidenced by the social science course-taking patterns we found, the exposure of children of immigrants to the civic discourse touted in higher-level government and elective coursework may be limited. In the following chapter, we expand our analyses to investigate whether and how exposure to civic discourse through formal social science course-taking and other informal facets of schooling shapes students' future political participation. Here we would point out that the government and civics teachers we interviewed repeatedly stressed the impact of student discussions in government, civics, and elective courses on future political participation. Specifically, they emphasized that those students who could connect the course curriculum to their lived experiences were more likely to be politically involved in their community. In contrast, the participating history teachers discussed the importance of learning and understanding the historical content on which their classroom discussions were based. Although these teachers were a small, non-nationally representative sample, their input suggests that the impact of social science preparation is more nuanced than we were able to measure through accumulated social science credits. Further research is necessary to improve our understanding of the nuances of the effects of different social science courses on civic and political participation.

In the following chapter, we investigate the association between students' social science preparation during high school and their political outcomes in young adulthood, particularly distinguishing the influence of social science courses and students' grades in these courses from the impact of their overall academic achievement and enrollment.

CHAPTER 6

Schools and the Political Participation
of Children of Immigrants

In prior chapters, we discussed immigrant political participation, academic preparation, and schooling at the start of the twenty-first century, as well as the impact of these factors on young adults' political participation. We have explored a number of ways in which schools may contribute to adolescents' political development and their early adult political participation, with an eye toward the unique situation of adolescent children of immigrants as they become young adults. In this chapter, we examine the relationship of high school experiences to actual political outcomes during early adulthood.

Formal and Informal High School Processes
Shaping Young Adult Citizens

We ask our questions in this chapter through the lens of the school as a receiving community for children of immigrants. For instance, what contributes to students' successful transition into their roles as adult citizens in this new century? In doing so, we address the relationship between the formal academic dimension of schooling and its informal social dimensions, and the relationship of both dimensions to early adult political participation, paying special attention to the differences in these experiences for children of immigrants. We close the chapter with a discussion of the role of school at the turn of the century, first for all students and then for immigrant youth in particular as they transition into young adulthood.

In investigating whether the formal courses that students take and their grades in those courses predict their level of political participation in early adulthood, we distinguish between social science courses and other academic courses where access is more stratified. We also consider whether the informal social dimensions of the school, representing the students' connection to the institution of the school, also promote political participation. Finally, we ask whether school experiences have a greater overall impact on children of immigrants.

FORMAL SCHOOLING: CITIZENSHIP EDUCATION

Social science courses expose students to the tenets of civic society and the importance, rewards, and responsibilities of individual participation in a healthy democracy. We know from previous research that adolescents' high school social science coursework is associated with their future political participation (Atherton 2000; Chaffee 2000; Niemi and Junn 1998). Here we extend this finding in two ways: First, we consider whether the effects of children of immigrants' exposure to social science coursework are similar to those observed for children of native-born parents. Second, we assess whether the relationship is part of a constellation of factors through which educational attainment and academic stratification and success contribute to future political participation, or whether something unique to social sciences courses promotes citizenship activities.

In chapter 4, we described stratification within schools that falls roughly along lines that separate course-taking in preparation for college among more academically advanced students from remediation for students with academic risk factors. Mathematics course placement is the best single indicator of such stratification (Adelman 1999). In chapter 5, we discussed the content of social sciences courses in general and especially how they relate to civics education. We now extend our investigation of these two elements of formal education to their impact on the future political engagement of children of immigrants and children of native-born parents.

Political knowledge has been linked to civic engagement and political participation in studies of high school and college-age youth. Specifically, political knowledge measured during adolescence predicts voting and other political activity during young adulthood (Sherrod 2003), as political knowledge is consistently associated with voting among adults (Delli Carpini and Keeter 1997). Although our quantitative data lack a measure of political or civic knowledge, researchers and educators alike point to the strong and robust association between social science coursework and the development of civic knowledge (Gamoran 1987; Leming 1996; Niemi and Junn 1998). We argue that for adolescent children of immigrants, social science coursework may prove especially important in shaping future political participation.

The teachers in our qualitative inquiry also pointed to the nebulous nature of civic outcomes in an era of accountability. Owing to federal (No Child Left Behind) and state-level end-of-course exams, student success is often discussed in terms of test scores rather than voting behavior, to many teachers' chagrin. Clearly, measuring the success of a high school social science program by the number of active young adult voters it produces in the future is not reasonable. Yet Mr. Tomasi, the San Diego history teacher, notes that "the problem with . . . getting . . . more civically conscious is that it's not something that can be tested." In fact, the pressure to focus on the test score in today's era of accountability proved quite frustrating to many teachers. Mr. Tomasi argued that, "if we're going to be civic-based . . . making people better citizens and getting involved, then there needs to be a more encompassing view of our role as opposed to just simple facts." Our analysis of the relationship between social science coursework and political participation in young adulthood sheds light on what exactly the role of schools and educators in the civic development of youth might be.

Students' grades in their social studies courses have been given less attention by researchers, but they are important to consider because they may reflect not only mastery of the course material but also students' enthusiasm for and engagement with the course topics. In other words, we might expect higher social science course grades to signify that a student has gained more knowledge, or that the knowledge gained is more salient, and in this way academic success in social science courses may foster enhanced political participation, either causally or because of the students' preexisting interest. For these reasons, we expect that students' future political activity may be positively predicted not only by their exposure to the content of the social science curriculum but also by their grades in their social science courses.

Although the quantity and quality of high school social science coursework may shape future political behaviors, it is important to remember that the high school social science curriculum is not necessarily an isolated influence; students' social positioning and socioeconomic status also affect the results of their education for citizenship (Parker 2001a). Although the impact of the social science curriculum is our primary interest in formal school processes, it is well documented that American high schools are highly stratified and that students' access to educational opportunities depends on family background and resources as well as their academic preparation and prior achievement (Gamoran 1987; Gamoran and Hannigan 2000; Lucas 1999; Oakes 1985). Demographic variation across U.S. schools suggests that the quality and quantity of the curriculum to which students, particularly children of immigrants, are exposed also varies (Cosentino de Cohen, Deterding, and Clewell 2005). Most research documenting the relationship between education and political participation uses indicators more closely aligned with overall academic achievement and attainment—in other words, indicators of academic status rather than an individual's knowledge of and interest in the political system.

Few studies addressing the link between social science coursework and political or civic knowledge take into account academic stratification, leaving open the question of whether the coursework-knowledge connection is a function of general stratification processes or would exist in the absence of stratification. Gamoran's (1987) study of high school learning opportunities did distinguish between the effects of exposure to civics courses and more general academic tracking and achievement; he found that civics courses were independently related to the generation of civic knowledge. We are unaware of any national study that links social science curricular exposure—independent from general academic status and attainment—to political participation.

How might the processes through which exposure to a social studies curriculum leads to enhanced political participation be different or unique for children of immigrants? To the extent that children of immigrants invest in schoolwork and value education more than children of native-born parents, we might expect an enhanced saliency of academic exposure among children of immigrants. As described in the previous chapter, social science as a topic may be more salient for children of immigrants because they bring cross-cultural experiences to the classroom and in this way have developed a more analytic lens for understanding the issues raised in the social sciences. An additional possibility relates to the intergenerational transmission of political knowledge and practices. Because adult immigrants' knowledge of the U.S. political process and their political participation are by definition relatively new and developing, transfers of knowledge and practices from this generation to the next may be more limited; where this is true, the saliency of school-based learning would be heightened for children of immigrants. Finally, the experiences of adolescent children of immigrants in bridging the worlds of home and school (Azmitia and Cooper 2001; Cooper et al. 2002; Valdés 1996) may predispose them to grasp the U.S.-based civics lessons in their social science coursework.

THE SOCIAL DIMENSION OF HIGH SCHOOLS

Evidence suggests that youths' political and civic engagement is local (Flanagan and Faison 2001; Sherrod et al. 2002), indicating the relevance of the social world of the school as a possible locus for the development of the political knowledge, understanding, and views of children of immigrants. Among American youth, identification with and participation in a larger social community predict civic integration (Delli Carpini 2000; Youniss, McLellan, and Yates 1997). As discussed in chapter 3, the high school is an important institution in American society, with defined boundaries within which adolescents develop a connection to community and a sense of belonging to a group outside the home and family. As an arena for the emergence of intense social interaction, the high school has the potential to influence the civic behaviors and choices of its students in early adulthood.

Among immigrant adults, civic engagement is increased when they belong to a group and participate in its organized activities (DeSipio 2002; Leal 2002). In fact, in general we find that adults' social integration and community connection shape their political participation (Putnam 2000). In this chapter, we investigate how adolescents' social connection to school promotes their future political participation. Among adolescent children of immigrants in particular, the role of social connection during adolescence in shaping adult political participation remains relatively unexplored.

Over the past decade, findings from the IEA Civic Education Study have helped to shape our understanding of the development of civic intent and knowledge. The IEA study includes over 140,000 fourteen-year-olds in twenty-eight countries and explores the relationship between the social science classroom and students' reported intent to participate in civic processes as adults (Torney-Purta et al. 2001). For our purposes, the IEA study is especially helpful because it takes the immigrant status of students into account, recognizing their potentially unique position in the social science classroom. For children of immigrants, as for the children of native-born parents, the researchers found that the academic emphasis of the school was associated with the development of students' civic knowledge (Torney-Purta 2002). Here the researchers operationalized academic emphasis as the degree to which other students in the school planned to pursue higher education, a measure of the academic rigor of the school community as a whole. These findings suggest the importance of the school climate in shaping young adult civic behaviors—including voting and registering to vote—for all students regardless of generational status.

In general, children of immigrants may attend schools that are less rigorous academically, have lower levels of peer performance and parental education, and provide less access to advanced courses (Dronkers and Levels 2007; Hao and Pong 2008; Schwartz and Steifel 2004). It is well documented that American high schools are stratified, both internally and with substantial disparities in access to quality curriculum between high schools (Lucas 1999; Muller et al. 2010; Oakes 1985; Stevenson et al. 1994). These disparities may be accompanied by socioeconomic differences in the families of a school's students; if so, this would partly explain the findings of Torney-Purta and her colleagues about differences in civic knowledge depending on the school climate and peers' overall academic performance at the school. Our analyses take this possibility into account.

In addition, many of the social science teachers in our qualitative inquiry were particularly aware of the question of peers' performance and the overall academic expectations in the social science classroom. Like Mr. Tomasi earlier in this chapter, several teachers reflected on whether they were making "good citizens" through their high academic standards. As Mr. Schroeder, a San Diego world history teacher, noted, he often reminded his students that advanced social science course-taking is "a privilege, not a right." In fact, he emphasized that his expectations were high because of the importance of developing "good citizens." Mr. Schroeder very much wanted his students to have a sense of responsibility that carries over into a social setting or a social responsibility because we do push that. You have to be educated. . . . We cover it with humanism and Confucianism, the importance of education. It's to make a better citizenry. So we're reinforcing that by lecturing about it, by getting them to do reports on education. And then for them to kind of reinforce that in their life, I think, yeah, it [developing good citizens] happens.

It is this intersection of the social science curriculum, high teacher expectations, and students' sense of obligation that may produce political participation later in life.

We turn now to our analysis of youths' political participation and socialization. We examine the effect of their experiences in high school as well as their social background in shaping whether as young adults they register to vote and whether they vote. In a separate analysis, we consider whether school experiences influence young adults' identification with a political party. Our interest lies in young adults' identification with any political party, not in their particular affiliations with the Democratic or Republican Party (or any other party). Children socialized by their families to identify with a particular party may be more likely to be taught critical thinking and even a passion for the democratic process in their school. Thus, it is possible that schools foster independent thinking. On the other hand, it may be that a student's passion for the political process leads to adopting a party identification. We explore these possibilities. For each of these indicators of political participation—registering to vote, voting, and party identification—we consider the possibility that the effects of experiences at school are different for children of immigrants compared to the experiences of children of native-born parents.

Registering to Vote, Voting, and Party Identification: Results

The bivariate statistics shown in table 6.1 suggest that children of immigrants were less likely to register to vote than children of native-born parents (71 percent compared to 76 percent); similarly, they were somewhat less likely to vote in the 2000 presidential election (43 percent compared to 46 percent). However, we found no meaningful difference in the likelihood of identifying with a political party (34 percent compared to 35 percent). Children of immigrants were more likely to have parents with lower educational levels and to have lower verbal scores on the AH-PVT (the PVT as abbreviated by Add Health) compared to children of native-born parents. In addition, children of immigrants took more advanced math but fewer social science courses than their native-born peers. As we saw in chapter 4, the Asian immigrant population is responsible for the higher levels of advanced math course-

Table 6.1   Proportions or Means and Standard Deviations (Weighted) for Analytic Sample, by Generational Status

Variable	Analytic Sample (N = 10,964)	Children of Native-Born (N = 8,954)	Children of Immigrants (N = 2,010)	Significant Difference
Outcomes				
Voter registration	0.75	0.76	0.71	**
Voted in 2000 election	0.45	0.46	0.43	
Identifies with a political party	0.35	0.35	0.34	
Background				
Female	0.49	0.49	0.48	
Asian	0.03	0.01	0.22	***
Black	0.16	0.18	0.06	***
Mexican Latino	0.06	0.03	0.23	***
Non-Mexican Latino	0.04	0.02	0.19	***
Other	0.03	0.03	0.05	†
Religious service attendance	0.76	0.75	0.78	
Parent education	3.53	3.59	3.12	**
	(1.67)	(1.60)	(2.00)	
AH-PVT verbal score	102.63	103.09	99.53	**
	(13.75)	(13.37)	(15.72)	
Formal and informal education				
Highest math taken	6.05	6.00	6.41	**
	(1.98)	(1.98)	(1.94)	
Social science credits	3.47	3.48	3.40	
	(1.44)	(1.45)	(1.39)	
Social science GPA	2.43	2.42	2.48	
	(1.01)	(1.02)	(0.97)	
Social connection to school	3.76	3.75	3.78	
	(0.88)	(0.88)	(0.84)	
Volunteering	0.43	0.43	0.47	†

Source: Add Health (Bearman et al. 1997) and AHAA (Muller et al. 2007).
Note: Means with standard deviations in parentheses.
†$p < .10$; **$p < .01$; ***$p < .001$

taking among immigrants; in general, Latino immigrants take fewer advanced mathematics courses than their non-Latino peers (Riegle-Crumb 2006; Tate 1997). Compared to their schoolmates, children of immigrants were also significantly more likely to have volunteered.

REGISTERING TO VOTE

Registering to vote is a basic form of electoral engagement; it is the first step taken to exercise the right to vote. Voter registration is a rite of passage to adulthood in the United States. Several high school civics teachers in our interview sample talked about the importance of publicly marking youths' transition into adult civic society: Ms. Jewel, the Chicago civics teacher, said: "When they turn eighteen, I hand them a voter registration card and say, 'Happy birthday.' Yeah. They love it. They're like, 'This is so lame. You don't have to be such a dork about it.' But they love it." Similarly, Mr. Rocca, the European history teacher in Florida, discussed a program that was invited into his school with the express purpose of publicizing this political coming-of-age experience:

> There is a program called Kids Voting . . . the voter registration office actually comes on campus, and they set up in the media center, the library, and the kids that, when they get to be seventeen, they can register to vote. . . . So when they show up, all of us who teach any social studies course are always on the kids . . . "How easy can it be? . . . All you have to do is go in there and fill out the card and you are registered to vote, and then when you turn eighteen, you are all good to go."

This very public recognition of an important rite of passage may be one way in which teachers and educators convey the civic outcomes expected of young adults in U.S. society. Teachers' efforts to make public the pathway to active citizenry may be particularly resonant for children of immigrants, whose parents by definition did not come of age in the U.S. system.

In fact, several immigrant young adults in our sample discussed their involvement in the voter registration process as young adults on their college campuses. Rosita, a young Latina from Florida, was quite enthusiastic about her role in helping other students register to vote. She reported with pride that she "ran a huge voting registration drive last year before the elections here on campus [through] a student nonpartisan organization." Like many of her peers, Rosita was probably influenced by the contentious Florida presidential race in 2000, which drove home the importance of each individual vote and was one factor in the upturn in the youth vote in 2004. Overall, Rosita and her colleagues "registered about two thousand kids to vote." Social science teachers' efforts to publicize this civic rite of passage appear to resonate with immigrant young adults like Rosita who come of political age in the United States.

Registering to vote, however, is shaped not only by teachers' encouragement but also by a number of other school and background factors. Along with individual characteristics, a number of school-related factors shape an individual's probability of registering to vote. Table 6.2 shows results from our logistic models predicting voter registration among U.S. citizens.[1] Beginning with model 1, where social background is held constant, we found no statistically significant difference in the likelihood of registering to vote when comparing the children of immigrants and their schoolmates whose parents were born in the United States. Consistent with prior research, we found that African Americans were about 81 percent more likely (1.81 = exp [0.592]) than whites to register to vote, and Asian Americans were about 33 percent less likely (0.325 = 1 − exp [−0.394]) than whites to do so. As we might expect, model 1 also shows that young adults who had higher verbal aptitude scores (AH-PVT), who attended church services, and whose parents had higher levels of education were also more likely to register to vote.

In model 2, we begin to explore the association of both formal and informal high school experiences with voter registration, using measures of course-taking and achievement and of social connection to the school. Students in more advanced math courses in high school, an indicator of college preparation, were slightly more likely to register to vote as young adults. Independent of college preparation, the number of social science credits taken in high school predicts future voter registration, and the higher a student's social science grades, the more likely that student will be to register to vote as a young adult. In our study, students who earned higher grades in social science courses were more likely to register; an increase of one grade point—from a C to a B, or from a B to an A—resulted in an 18 percent increase in the odds of registering. Our multinomial regression results (not shown) indicate that the significant estimated effects of social science credits and grades are due mainly to the strong positive relationship between these indicators and voting; social science credits and social science grades do not predict who will register to vote if they do not actually vote.

Informal school experiences are also associated with voter registration. Adolescents who felt connected to their high school or who volunteered during high school were more likely to register to vote. Our estimates suggest that those who volunteered during high school were about 69 percent more likely to register than schoolmates who did not. Consistent with the observed bivariate statistics, even with the inclusion of formal and informal school experiences, the estimated overall difference in the likelihood of registering to vote remains nonsignificant between children of immigrants and their schoolmates.

We also seek to understand whether these relationships are different for children of immigrants. In model 3, we included interaction terms between immigrant status and (1) parents' education level and (2) the number of social science credits taken as an adolescent. These interaction terms estimated whether the effect on registration of background or high school experiences is different between children of immigrants and children of native-born par-

Table 6.2 Logistic Regression Predicting Voter Registration in Young Adulthood

Registered, Did Not Vote	Model 1		Model 2		Model 3		Model 4	
Level 1 (student)								
Intercept	−3.660	(0.495)***	−4.532	(0.557)***	−4.538	(0.558)***	−6.661	(1.320)***
Background								
Immigrant	0.009	(0.105)	−0.104	(0.105)	−0.125	(0.108)	−0.100	(0.112)
Female	0.009	(0.066)	−0.114	(0.066)†	−0.108	(0.066)	−0.095	(0.067)
Asian	−0.394	(0.174)*	−0.561	(0.174)**	−0.529	(0.177)**	−0.470	(0.182)*
Black	0.592	(0.133)***	0.625	(0.127)***	0.632	(0.128)***	0.606	(0.126)***
Mexican Latino	0.149	(0.159)	0.178	(0.165)	0.147	(0.174)	0.226	(0.177)
Non-Mexican Latino	0.093	(0.128)	0.109	(0.134)	0.096	(0.133)	0.200	(0.159)
Other	−0.179	(0.173)	−0.120	(0.177)	−0.121	(0.179)	−0.044	(0.187)
Parent education level	0.231	(0.023)***	0.167	(0.024)***	0.187	(0.026)***	0.170	(0.027)***
Age	0.126	(0.025)***	0.158	(0.026)***	0.158	(0.026)***	0.167	(0.025)***
AH-PVF score	0.016	(0.003)***	0.007	(0.003)*	0.007	(0.003)*	0.006	(0.003)*
Religious service attendance	0.425	(0.072)***	0.243	(0.073)**	0.241	(0.074)**	0.210	(0.074)**
Formal and informal schooling								
Highest math taken			0.067	(0.025)**	0.067	(0.025)**	0.069	(0.025)**
Social science credits			0.053	(0.030)†	0.029	(0.030)	0.025	(0.030)

	Model 1	Model 2	Model 3
Social science GPA	0.169 (0.053)**	0.167 (0.053)**	0.151 (0.051)**
Social connection to school	0.154 (0.040)***	0.159 (0.040)***	0.152 (0.040)***
Volunteered	0.526 (0.075)***	0.522 (0.075)***	0.526 (0.076)***
Interaction terms			
Immigrant*Parent Education		−0.109 (0.044)*	−0.108 (0.046)*
Immigrant*Social Science Credits		0.198 (0.073)**	0.203 (0.074)**
Level 2 (school)			
South			0.187 (0.102)†
Private			−0.178 (0.208)
Parent education level			0.184 (0.079)*
Proportion immigrant			−0.131 (0.220)
Social connection			0.394 (0.298)

Source: Add Health (Bearman et al. 1997) and AHAA (Muller et al. 2007).

Note: Sample size = 10,913 students. Unstandardized coefficients are shown with robust standard errors in parentheses.

† $p < .10$; * $p < .05$; ** $p < .01$; *** $p < .001$

ents. Our exploratory analyses indicated that the estimated effects of these two variables differ significantly for children of native-born parents and children of immigrants. More specifically, model 3 indicates that the observed positive effect of parents' education level in predicting registration pertains only to children of native-born parents. Among children of immigrants, parents' level of education did not predict registration.[2] In contrast, children of native-born parents from more-educated families were more likely to participate in politics; this was not true of children of immigrants.

Turning to formal school experiences, we hypothesize that when children of immigrants accumulate more social science credits, they are more likely to register to vote in young adulthood compared to children of U.S.-born parents. For children of immigrants, formal schooling—in this case, social science course-taking—matters more than it does for the children of native-born parents. Social science course-taking is a significant predictor of voter registration in young adulthood among children of immigrants, confirming the civic role of schools in producing new citizens for a new century.

VOTING IN THE 2000 PRESIDENTIAL ELECTION

Prior to the 2000 election, much attention was paid to the youth vote. MTV launched a campaign to "Rock the Vote" as part of a nationwide initiative to encourage political participation among young adults, including children of immigrant parents (Cloonan and Street 1998; López et al. 2006). Following a period of relative decline in the youth vote, the rate of registration as well as the rate of voting among young adults age eighteen to twenty-four (the target age group of the present study) rose above 50 percent in the 2000 election (Jamieson, Shin, and Day 2002). The youth vote remained strong in the 2008 election as well; however, the spike in 2004 is often attributed to a heightened sensitivity to the importance of each individual vote following Florida's close electoral contest in 2000, as well as to concerns about the Iraq War. Several of our young adult respondents commented on the important role of the youth vote, especially in a tight election. Genaro, the second-generation Cuban-Dominican student from New York, emphasized the importance of voting to his peers at college: "I told people, 'Let's go vote,' [especially] friends who didn't know what was the point of voting; I told them how Pennsylvania for one is a swing state." This kind of strong commitment to voting in their larger communities—to ensuring a voice for themselves and their peers—was echoed throughout our interviews. Youths' enthusiasm in the most recent elections reflects the more general trends we uncovered in our quantitative study.

Specifically, the strength of the youth vote is reflected again in the voting patterns in Add Health. Table 6.3 shows the high school experiences and social background factors that predicted who would vote in the 2000 presidential election, which occurred just prior to wave 3 data collection in 2001. Overall, the models predicting voting are similar to those that predict voter registration, in part because voter registration is a precondition for voting. Where registering to vote is essentially a passive act (for example, checking a box when obtaining a driver's license), the act of voting in the presidential election represents a higher form of electoral engagement.

Although our focus remains on how schools shape political participation, we note that the background determinants of voting are similar to those observed for registering to vote. We found no differences between children of immigrant and children of native-born parents in whether they voted in the 2000 presidential election. Asians were less likely to vote and African Americans more likely, once other background factors were held constant. Parental education was a strong predictor of voting, as was students' verbal ability, as measured by the PVT.

School experiences were also related to who voted in early adulthood. Students who earned higher social studies GPAs, who took more social science courses, and who volunteered while in high school were all more likely to have voted as young adults. The multinomial model (not shown) indicates that students who took more advanced math courses were also more likely to vote. In addition, students who reported a stronger social connection to their high school were more active in electoral politics as young adults.

Similar to our findings on voter registration, our results suggest that schools maintain a crucial role among children of immigrants. The interaction terms—where the effects of parents' education and social science credits were estimated separately for children of immigrants—indicated that parents' education did not predict voting among children of immigrants, whereas social science credits did predict whether they would vote. These estimated effects were stronger in the multinomial model, where voters were contrasted with only nonregistered nonvoters. Although parents' education level largely predicted voting among the children of native-born parents, it had no such effect on voting among children of immigrants. Here we see very clearly the critical role of formal schooling, as expressed by social science course-taking, on the future political participation of adolescent children of immigrants.

Because these interaction terms are difficult to interpret, we present them in graphical form as predicted probabilities of voting. The line graphs in figures 6.1 and 6.2 show expected levels of political participation for otherwise "average" respondents while simultaneously illustrating the differences according to parental nativity. Because parents' level of education is an ordinal rather than an interval variable, we also estimated the relationship using dummy variables, with similar results. We present estimates with a single variable for parental education level for parsimony. At moderate levels of parental education, there was virtually no difference between the groups in the probability that they would register or vote in early adulthood. The difference

Table 6.3 Logistic Regression Predicting Voting in Young Adulthood

Voted	Model 1		Model 2		Model 3		Model 4	
Level 1 (student)								
Intercept	-5.134	(0.425)***	-6.195	(0.457)***	-6.204	(0.462)***	-8.910	(0.949)***
Background								
Immigrant	0.119	(0.094)	0.044	(0.098)	0.019	(0.098)	-0.003	(0.101)
Female	0.078	(0.057)	-0.033	(0.060)	-0.030	(0.060)	-0.019	(0.058)
Asian	-0.369	(0.157)*	-0.490	(0.163)**	-0.448	(0.173)*	-0.469	(0.184)*
Black	0.655	(0.119)***	0.720	(0.117)***	0.727	(0.116)***	0.708	(0.119)***
Mexican Latino	0.152	(0.129)	0.200	(0.132)	0.158	(0.138)	0.154	(0.135)
Non-Mexican Latino	0.050	(0.111)	0.072	(0.111)	0.046	(0.112)	0.053	(0.137)
Other	-0.098	(0.148)	-0.045	(0.147)	-0.036	(0.146)	0.012	(0.148)
Parent education level	0.197	(0.018)***	0.140	(0.019)***	0.156	(0.021)***	0.131	(0.022)***
Age	0.118	(0.020)***	0.149	(0.021)***	0.149	(0.021)***	0.161	(0.022)***
AH-PVT score	0.019	(0.003)***	0.010	(0.003)***	0.010	(0.003)***	0.010	(0.003)**
Religious service attendance	0.442	(0.070)***	0.271	(0.070)***	0.270	(0.071)***	0.248	(0.071)***
Formal and informal schooling								
Highest math taken			0.040	(0.025)	0.041	(0.025)	0.040	(0.025)
Social science credits			0.074	(0.027)**	0.058	(0.026)*	0.053	(0.025)*

	Model 1		Model 2		Model 3	
Social science GPA	0.187	(0.040)***	0.185	(0.040)***	0.175	(0.039)***
Social connection to school	0.180	(0.033)***	0.183	(0.033)***	0.169	(0.033)***
Volunteered	0.385	(0.062)***	0.382	(0.062)***	0.371	(0.062)***
Interaction terms						
Immigrant*Parent Education			−0.092	(0.041)*	−0.086	(0.043)*
Immigrant*Social Science Credits			0.134	(0.076)†	0.144	(0.078)†
Level 2 (school)						
South					0.106	(0.080)
Private					−0.088	(0.134)
Parent education level					0.182	(0.060)**
Proportion immigrant					0.229	(0.225)
Social connection					0.562	(0.192)**

Source: Add Health (Bearman et al. 1997) and AHAA (Muller et al. 2007).

Note: Sample size = 10,914 students. Unstandardized coefficients are shown with robest standard errors in parentheses.

†$p < .10$; *$p < .05$; **$p < .01$; ***$p < .001$

Figure 6.1.   Association Between Parental Education and Voting and Registering to Vote in Young Adulthood, by Generation

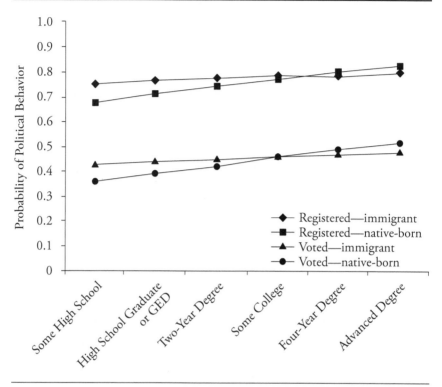

Source: Authors' calculations from Add Health (Bearman et al. 1997) and AHAA (Muller et al. 2007).

between the two groups increased as parents' education increased. Children of more highly educated native-born parents had higher levels of political participation, while parents' education was unrelated to political participation among the children of immigrants. Similarly, children of less-educated native-born parents were especially unlikely to vote.

In contrast, we found that some school experiences predict the political behaviors of children of immigrants, but not the behaviors of children of native-born parents. Again comparing otherwise average students, children of immigrants who accumulated more social science credits in high school tended to be more likely to register and to vote (figure 6.2). The estimated differences between the two groups were relatively small among students with few social science credits, but the gap widened considerably around three or four credits. This represents about one course per year, which is the

Figure 6.2.   Association Between Social Science Credits and Voting and Registering to Vote in Young Adulthood, by Generation

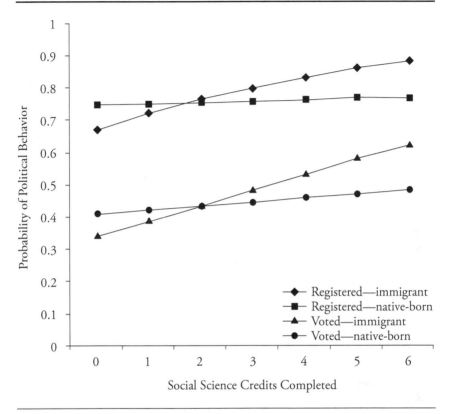

Source: Authors' calculations from Add Health (Bearman et al. 1997) and AHAA (Muller et al. 2007).

average amount of social science required for high school in most schools and states. The children of immigrants who accumulated more than four social science credits were more than six percentage points more likely to register to vote and then to vote than the children of native-born parents. The gap emerged because children of immigrants were more likely to register and to vote when they took more social science, but a similar relationship did not exist among children of native-born parents.

In exploring the relationship between school context and the political development of all students, later young adults, we drew from a national sample of high schools in the Add Health data set. Across all schools and all adolescents, those students who attended schools with relatively higher average levels of parental education were more likely to register and to vote than to do neither. Here our findings suggest that the role of parents' education—and most likely other aspects related to the socioeconomic status of families served by the school—extends beyond individual families and into the larger school community as a whole; higher levels of parental education at a school benefit all students, even when an individual student's parents have little formal education. Ancillary analyses (not shown) indicate that children of immigrants and children of native-born parents experienced the effects of peers' parental education levels in the same ways.

In addition to a student's individual social connection, we found that the connection of their peers to the school was positively associated with young adults' future voting. Students who attended high schools where the student body felt more connected to the school were more likely to vote as young adults. These differences suggest the benefits of creating a sense of connection to the school community that can promote political participation in young adulthood. Our analysis includes results (not shown) indicating that the effect of social connection at the school level was related to the voting behavior of immigrant young adults and the children of native-born parents in similar ways.

Party Identification

The final form of electoral engagement that we examine is identification with a political party, which is distinct from political participation, voting, and registering to vote in many ways. Nearly half a century ago, Kent Jennings and Richard Niemi (1968) documented the direct transmission of political values from parent to child in the American-born population, leaving little room for the influence of school or community factors. Further research focused on non-native-born, nonwhite populations has indicated, however, that the issue of party identification is much more complex (Wong and Tseng 2007). In fact, Janelle Wong (2000) finds that political exposure rather than family patterns explains partisan choices among immigrant groups. And in a recent examination of current patterns of political identification, Zoltan Hajnal and Taeku Lee (2011) argue that party identification is shaped by factors that elicit varied responses from different racial and ethnic groups, causing patterns of engagement to diverge even further.

In contrast to voting behavior, children of immigrants were more likely to report identifying with a political party when compared with children of native-born parents. Not surprisingly, our ancillary analyses indicated that children of immigrants were more likely to identify as Democrat. Similarly, African American young adults were more likely than whites to identify with a political party (and to identify as a Democrat). Asian-origin students were less likely to report a party identification. Students whose parents had higher levels of education, those who attended church, and those who went to school in the South were more likely to identify with a political party. Our ancillary analyses suggested that students who attended church more often and those from the South also showed higher levels of affiliation with the Republican Party.

The school experiences associated with party identification appear to be less centered on coursework and more on social experiences, confirming Hajnal and Lee's (2011) argument connecting partisan identification to social identity and ideology. Students' grades (but not their social studies credits or their mathematics placement) predicted whether they would identify with a political party. It is possible that the higher-performing students in social science were the ones most engaged in the material, both while they were in high school and afterward. In analyses not shown, we explored whether the relationship was simply a function of higher-achieving students being more likely to identify with a political party; we found that social science GPA was a better predictor of party identification than overall GPA or GPA in all academic courses—a finding that confirmed prior findings regarding the role of information in shaping party identification among immigrants (Hajnal and Lee 2011). Students' social connection to school and their volunteer work while in high school were also associated with party identification in early adulthood—another confirmation of the importance of identity and ideology.

In our final models, we estimated whether the young adult identified with any political party (compared to no identification). However, in models not shown, we also estimated identification as a Democrat and separately as a Republican and reported those results where relevant. Table 6.4 shows the results from nested logistic regressions that predict party identification with the same set of variables used in tables 6.2 and 6.3 to predict voter registration and voting, respectively. In contrast to our models predicting voting and voter registration, we found no differences between children of immigrant and native-born parents in any of the relationships between background or school experiences and identification with a political party. In other words, when it comes to social background effects and factors in high school that shape political party identification in early adulthood, children of immigrants and children of native-born parents are remarkably similar.

Several key points related to party identification surfaced in our qualitative analyses and bear mention at this point. First, several of our target social science teachers discussed their efforts to be objective in the classroom. Teachers' views on nonpartisanship reflected not only a pedagogical position but also very real constraints on partisan advocacy by teachers as public employees. In addition to these external constraints, teachers' decisions about presenting partisan ideals were also influenced by the impressionable nature of their students, by their own professionalism, and by a strong sense of responsibility, especially toward the children of immigrants. Mr. Jones, the U.S. history teacher in Florida, said:

Table 6.4 Logistic Regression Predicting Identification with a Political Party in Young Adulthood

Variables	Model 1		Model 2		Model 3		Model 4	
Level 1 (student)								
Intercept	-3.923	(0.426)***	-4.74	(0.486)***	-4.764	(0.490)***	-5.461	(1.251)***
Background								
Immigrant	0.267	(0.111)*	0.203	(0.108)†	0.196	(0.104)†	0.195	(0.110)†
Female	0.119	(0.056)*	0.008	(0.058)	0.009	(0.058)	0.029	(0.058)
Asian	-0.655	(0.223)**	-0.765	(0.222)***	-0.737	(0.223)**	-0.758	(0.205)***
Black	0.572	(0.120)***	0.651	(0.114)***	0.657	(0.115)***	0.612	(0.124)***
Mexican Latino	-0.084	(0.140)	-0.049	(0.139)	-0.091	(0.141)	-0.097	(0.145)
Non–Mexican Latino	0.065	(0.159)	0.087	(0.173)	0.072	(0.167)	0.051	(0.177)
Other	-0.188	(0.197)	-0.150	(0.194)	-0.143	(0.193)	-0.156	(0.199)
Parent education level	0.161	(0.023)***	0.105	(0.023)***	0.115	(0.025)***	0.114	(0.020)***
Age	0.049	(0.022)*	0.073	(0.023)**	0.073	(0.023)**	0.076	(0.024)**
AH–PVF score	0.014	(0.003)***	0.006	(0.003)*	0.006	(0.003)*	0.007	(0.003)*
Religious service attendance	0.444	(0.076)***	0.286	(0.076)***	0.284	(0.075)***	0.237	(0.076)**

Formal and informal schooling			
Highest math taken	0.020 (0.022)	0.020 (0.022)	0.019 (0.021)
Social science credits	0.025 (0.027)	0.022 (0.028)	0.012 (0.028)
Social science GPA	0.230 (0.041)***	0.229 (0.041)***	0.225 (0.037)***
Social connection to school	0.164 (0.036)***	0.164 (0.036)***	0.150 (0.036)***
Volunteered	0.420 (0.069)***	0.418 (0.069)***	0.420 (0.069)***
Interaction terms			
Immigrant*Parent Education		−0.057 (0.043)	−0.053 (0.043)
Immigrant*Social Science Credits		0.022 (0.072)	0.027 (0.076)
Level 2 (school)			
South			0.200 (0.097)*
Private			0.509 (0.152)**
Parent education level			−0.020 (0.068)
Proportion immigrant			0.043 (0.242)
Social connection			0.188 (0.278)

Source: Add Health (Bearman et al. 1997) and AHAA (Muller et al. 2007).

Note: Sample size = 10,852 students. Unstandardized coefficients are shown with robust standard errors in parentheses.

†$p < .10$; *$p < .05$; **$p < .01$; ***$p < .001$

I want to be careful to . . . portray objectivity because . . . the students are very malleable and can be shaped. If I present that Obama is bad, bad, bad, or Bush is good, good, good, or any of those things, [my students] are going to get a warped perspective . . . and I think the media does a fantastic job of that already. So I am . . . very sensitive and very selective about how I want to use something with President Obama per se. . . . I want to be clear with them, I want to present both sides. . . . Students interpret things in a wide variety of ways; the way things come out of your mouth aren't necessarily interpreted the way you intended them.

Many of the teachers described exercises and activities they used to help their students not only recognize but also analyze their beliefs to determine where they fell on the political spectrum. The Florida teacher Mr. Rocca had this to say:

You would think that kids would have a clearer conception of their political self . . . by the time they get to be seventeen years old, but it is amazing how many don't. . . . [So] we try to get them to articulate their political beliefs, so that when they go in there, they can register with the party that is most consistent with what they believe, knowing of course that they can always change their party affiliation.

This is not to suggest that social science teachers never expressed their views. In fact, several explicitly recognized their position as a model for political decision-making, especially with their immigrant students. Ms. Martínez, the Texas history teacher, elaborated on this process, noting that she did not share it with the whole class, but rather with students on a one-on-one basis.

I don't blurt out my political beliefs, *ever.* But if a student comes and asks me a question, I'm happy to give [the student] my input. You have to do it without judgment, which I think might be what they don't get at home. So, as they are beginning to formulate, "What is it that I believe in?" having someone say, "I believe this because of this" [is helpful]. And that's almost never done in class, it's almost always done after lecture; they come in at lunchtime. "Can we talk about this?" "Sure." And then we elaborate on that.

Ms. Martínez, like many of her colleagues, recognized the importance of modeling how an adult evaluates evidence to make a decision about a political issue. Like most of the social science teachers in our study, however, she worked hard not to insist that one particular point of view was always right. This is not to say that teachers never express political opinions—many do— but rather that, as our quantitative and qualitative data findings suggest, their goal is to encourage students simply to identify with a party, not to steer them toward identification with a particular party.

The Latino young adults we interviewed appreciated and respected their teachers' efforts to raise their partisan awareness. Although many, not surprisingly, identified with one party or another most of the time, several spoke specifically to their right to change allegiance depending on the views of particular candidates. Ramiro, a twenty-year-old Florida student of Cuban origin, said that one of his teachers

> taught us to be well rounded. He always said to never pick a side, don't label yourself as Democratic, don't label yourself as Republican, label you as you. You vote for who you believe is going to be the right person to vote for, the person who is going to make a change that you feel is the right change that our country needs. So having that mentality really helps, especially with the . . . current election, the 2008 election. I voted for who I felt was going to . . . take the action that I felt would lead our country to a better place.

Similarly, Juan, also from Florida, noted that "right now I can say I am involved with the Democrats, but if a Republican candidate comes tomorrow with something that feels for me I will probably follow him. . . . I don't like the party lines." This partisan independence is reiterated in our models predicting identification with a political party in general, but not necessarily with one party over another in our statistical models. Our immigrant young adults reflected both the partisanship and the objectivity of their social science teachers as they made their own political decisions in young adulthood.

Conclusions

Taken together, our results suggest a central role of high school social science in the political socialization of all adolescents, and of children of immigrants in particular. Not only did we find that social science coursework plays an important role in predicting voting and registering to vote among children of immigrants, but we also found that two other aspects of schooling, volunteering and social connection to the school, predict identification with a political party in young adulthood. In addition, our qualitative analyses flesh out the role of social science teachers in the political decision-making of their former immigrant students. Just as other scholars have found that children of immigrants value school and are high achievers, we found that children of immigrants appear to make the most of their civic and political education in high school.

Compared to children of native-born parents, children of immigrants appear to gain relatively more from their school experiences, in particular their social science coursework. Importantly, our analytic approach took into ac-

count students' academic achievement overall, across content areas, in pars-
ing and estimating the specific effects related to social science coursework. In
the next chapter, we discuss in greater depth the implications of these findings for the schooling and education of children of immigrants, a growing
segment of the voting population.

CHAPTER 7

Conclusions and Implications: Adolescent Children of Immigrants and Their Schools

I think the problem with getting more civically conscious—it's not something that can be tested . . . taxpayers don't care about that [civic development] at this point. I mean, ideally they'd like to see . . . would they like to see everybody vote? . . . [Well,] that's up for grabs.

—Mr. Tomasi, world history teacher, San Diego

We began this study with the premise that high schools are important venues for adolescents' political development, providing experiences that help them become active in our nation's democratic process. Schools not only prepare young people for labor force participation but also socialize them in important ways to become independent adults who contribute to their communities and the larger society in both thought and action. We hypothesized that children of immigrant parents find their school experiences particularly salient; that they typically embrace school opportunities; and that exposure to new ideas through social science and politics coursework resonates for them as they navigate the dual cultures of family and community. Indeed, many of the teachers we spoke with described their goal of conveying a sense of opportunity and empowerment to their students, and students, in turn, often described their favorite teachers as those who gave them a better sense of what was possible. Our empirical data support these hypotheses about the role of high school in shaping the early adult political activity of students, especially children of immigrants.

We argue that schools may matter now more than ever before. In chapter 1, we illustrated the nationwide demographic and geographic shifts driven by the young and growing population of children of immigrants. We argue that these changes have implications for the political future of the United States, and our focus on schools and schooling directly addresses one critical point in the future of the nation: political engagement. More specifically, our work reveals the significant, positive relationship between social science coursetaking and voting among children of immigrants. This finding speaks to the potential incorporation—or disenfranchisement—of a growing segment of the American population. Immigrant young adults coming of civic age in our nation's high schools constitute the heart of America's democracy.

Importantly, social studies coursework appears to promote voting among children of immigrants independent of the well-documented relationship between educational attainment and voting; thus, the political socialization of children of immigrants becomes all the more relevant, especially with the immigrant diaspora in recent years, documented in chapter 1. Children of immigrants are now represented in schools, districts, and states across the nation, and our findings suggest that schools can and do directly promote political participation among this growing population of children of immigrants through social science course-taking. Access to the social science curriculum and content has become a question of enfranchisement of youth across a variety of sectors of our society. Local constituencies hoping to maintain their political representation will do well to ensure access to the social science curriculum and content for their growing populations of children of immigrants, the voters of tomorrow.

Unlike racial and ethnic minorities, we found that children of immigrants as a whole do not demonstrate any particular political partisanship. Rather, they vote along family, ethnic, and community lines. Much of the immigrant literature focuses on family and community; we chose to explore a relatively less well documented context, the school. Although ultimately their schooling predicts *whether* children of immigrants will vote, *how* they might identify politically appears to be more a function of their community and ethnic identification. For example, Latino and black immigrants tend to identify as Democrat, as do their third-plus-generation peers. Children of immigrants and children of native-born parents may approach the process of party identification quite differently. Hajnal and Lee (2011), for instance, in their examination of partisan identification among adult voters, demonstrate that Latinos and Asians respond quite differently to identity, ideology, and information than black or white Americans: for Latinos and Asians, the decision not to identify with a specific party may be a rational response. Our findings about immigrant students' political identification aligning with their community and ethnicity are consistent with the more general observation that culture and ethnicity matters, and indeed matters more than immigrant generational status, for shaping many dimensions of adolescents' development, including identity (Kasinitz et al. 2009). How the process of party identification functions among children of immigrants once race is taken into account merits further exploration. While the schools do not promote a particular political party perspective but rather provide children of immigrants with the skills to take on the civic responsibilities of citizenship, young voters are nevertheless likely to vote to represent their communities.

If schools and districts curtail their social science programs, they will effectively curtail the political and civic engagement of the next generation of voters in their school population. Curricular access leads to children of immigrants' enfranchisement and opens the pathways to voting in young adulthood for these relatively new citizens. Thus, it is important to face the implications of reducing or eliminating social science programs for the future of U.S. civic society during an era of accountability (Rock et al. 2006; VanFossen 2005): deemphasizing these programs at the local level in response to federal and state accountability requirements could result over the long term in the diminished civic and political involvement of a generation of citizens.

Early on in this study, after we had published an article connecting social science course-taking to voting among children of immigrants, we received a phone call from an educator in a large district that was considering a reduction in the social science curriculum and high school graduation requirements because students were not tested on that curriculum under the state's accountability program. Administrators were concerned that time and energy dedicated to the social science curriculum would hurt the state's Race to the Top rankings. An academic as well as a civic argument can be made, however, for the protection of the social science curriculum: American youth, and children of immigrants in particular, may benefit from the academic content of these courses, and American society depends on the civic identity developed in these courses. Our study suggests that state and local education agencies, in reducing their social science curriculum, may be compromising their political representation in the long run.

Schools and Citizenship

As we see in the association between social science coursework and political participation, especially with respect to parental education, schools occupy a distinct space in the political development of children of immigrants. Parents' education level is certainly not an ideal proxy for political knowledge and interest, but it does offer one measure of preparation for civic life. Among children of native-born parents, parental education is strongly associated with future political participation, consistent with prior empirical work exploring political socialization in the home (Jennings and Niemi 1968; Jennings et al. 2009). However, we found no evidence of any such association among children of immigrants. Instead, high school social science preparation directly shapes the future political participation of children of immigrants. Schools and schooling are important for all students, but social science instruction is particularly important for children of immigrants.

The school makes a difference in adolescents' political activity as young adults in several ways: those who feel a greater connection to school, those who attend higher-SES schools, and those who are enrolled in schools with higher levels of social connection are all more likely to register to vote, to identify with a political party, and, most important, to turn out on election day. Our findings point to the central role that schools play in the political socialization of our growing population of immigrant youth. The direct transmission model of political participation that characterizes native-born families—one generation passing its political values along to the next—does not apply here (Bloemraad and Trost 2008; Wong and Tseng 2007). At the end of the day, immigrant parents will vary in how familiar they are with the U.S. political system and how much they trust it; for their children, what may consistently matter more for their future political participation is their school experience, and particularly the social science courses that they take.

IMMIGRANT YOUTH, SCHOOLS, AND CIVIC SOCIETY

With immigrant families increasingly responsible for population growth in our nation, the political socialization that occurs within the school has become even more important. Our work, in exploring the ways in which American high schools can cultivate future political participation and a democratic citizenry, has shown that high school social science courses will shape our future citizenry as this growing sector matures.

Although the academic and social aspects of schooling shape the civic and professional futures of all students to some extent, social science preparation is particularly crucial to the civic futures of children of immigrants. The variations we observed between children of immigrants and children of native-born parents in their social science preparation and informal school experiences, as well as the variations in the association of these school experiences with future political participation, may uniquely mark immigrant youth as they embark on their civic lives.

More than anything, we found that children of immigrants are just like their third-plus-generation peers as they transition into the peer-dominated society of adolescence and young adulthood. In a few very important ways, however, schools matter more in the civic development of children of immigrants. Social science preparation, especially the accumulation of credits and exposure to content, matters in a very concrete way in the civic development of immigrant youth. High school civics coursework in particular can contribute to the political socialization of these relatively new Americans. How schools evaluate and respond to the English-language proficiency of their immigrant language minority youth matters as well: these assessments set in motion sorting and stratifying mechanisms that have a significant impact on immigrant students' academic success. Although we found no direct relationship between ESL placement and social science course-taking, we did find a statistically significant estimated negative effect on math and science course-taking and math test scores among language minority youth. Any suppression of the overall academic achievement of immigrant language minority students may have an indirect, but important, impact on their future political participation: more academically prepared individuals are more likely to vote. Our results suggest that being placed in ESL lowers the likelihood that some immigrant language minority youths will prepare for college, much less go to college, and this narrowing of their academic opportunities may muffle their emergent civic voices.

In suggesting a very important role for schools in the political coming of age of the growing population of children of immigrants, our analysis does not discount the importance of families and communities, but rather points to the *additional* impact of schools. Through the academic and social facets of schooling, children of immigrants come of age politically in much the same way as children of native-born parents. They differ in one important respect, however: schools appear to ignite the strengths and skills that children of immigrants bring to the classroom, and this school experience encourages their political participation later in young adulthood.

THE FUNCTION OF SCHOOLING: POLITICAL OUTCOMES AND IMMIGRANT YOUTH

Although we found that high school experiences may be especially important for children of immigrants, it is important to note that schools do not appear to impart a partisan bias. Young adults who are academically successful in high school and those who leave high school better prepared for college are more likely to have a party identification, but that identification is not predictably Republican or Democrat. As our participants, teachers and students alike, repeatedly noted, it is most important for students to think independently and to make informed decisions. Social science coursework itself is not related to party identification; however, student-driven social experiences at the school do appear to matter—most notably volunteering and a sense of attachment to the school. These social experiences exert a similar influence on future political participation regardless of parental nativity. In offering adolescents avenues to independence and a variety of mentors and role models, volunteering and extracurricular involvement are crucial in the transition to adulthood. Again, such activity works similarly for children of immigrants and children of native-born parents alike. It is the formal aspect of schooling, social science course-taking, that differentially predicts political participation among children of immigrants. The social, academic, and civic aspects of schooling are equally critical to the central role of schools in the political socialization of children of immigrants.

WHAT DO SCHOOLS DO?

Schools have long acted as agents of social and cultural incorporation among children of immigrants (Goodlad 1984). One of the principal ways in which U.S. schools directly address the social and academic incorporation of children of immigrants is via English-language instruction for non-native English speakers. Schools' provision of linguistic support services serves not only to incorporate children of immigrants linguistically into the American culture but also to ensure their access to the academic content of science, math, and civics courses. Thus, language is intricately woven throughout the social, academic, and civic goals of schools and schooling. The various forms of language instruction in U.S. schools all ultimately shape the academic, social, and civic incorporation of the growing children of immigrants population.

The Academic Role of Schools   A major function of high schools is to prepare students for college and for the labor force. Although children of immigrants tend to perform well in school, they often are enrolled in lower-quality schools (Cortes 2006; Pong and Hao 2007; Schwartz and Steifel 2004), and some children of immigrants, especially those who take ESL courses over many years, may have fewer opportunities to learn (Callahan 2005; Callahan et al. 2010). Beyond the issue of access to good schools, within-school stratification (Lucas and Berends 2007; Muller et al. 2010) may also lower opportunities to learn for some children of immigrants and students of color. Because of the strong link between educational attainment and voting behavior, it is important to recognize that this stratification plays an important role in shaping the voting behavior of children of immigrants.

As measured by peers' parental education level, social connection to school, and social science performance, we can say that school context influences the political participation of immigrant and non-immigrant students alike. It was surprising to us that the proportion of children of immigrants present in the school was not associated with their future political participation, regardless of nativity. Given the resegregation evident in American schools today (Orfield 2001), a null effect in this area suggests that enrollment in immigrant-enclave schools is unlikely to limit the political participation of children of immigrants in the future, beyond the overall effects of quality schools. Thus, we can hope that immigrant-enclave communities, as well as outlying areas, will benefit from the leadership that children of immigrants are poised to take in their communities when schools effectively prepare them for college and professional occupations.

Similarly, the fact remains that individuals with higher levels of academic achievement and attainment are more likely to vote, whether children of native-born or immigrant parents. Our analyses disaggregated social science GPA from overall grades, and social science course-taking from overall college preparation, to find that civics instruction truly is the driving force behind political participation among children of immigrants. This is not to say that overall academic achievement and attainment are not critical; academic success remains hugely important for everyone, regardless of parental nativity. In addition, net of an individual student's own family background, schools with more highly educated parents have students who register and vote more as young adults. Perhaps in schools with higher levels of parental education more emphasis is put on political engagement and responsibility; alternatively, it may be some other, unmeasured factor—such as access to information, the quality of the curriculum, or unmeasured socioeconomic status—that is associated with future political behavior. However, it is important to note that these relationships are independent of the individual student's academic performance and family background. Future research might explore differences in schools' political and civic climates based on the socioeconomic composition of the school.

An underlying issue for one group of children of immigrants—those lacking legal documentation—is their access to higher education and a legitimate position in the workforce. Although eleven states have now passed legislation allowing academically successful undocumented children of immigrants to receive in-state tuition, thirty-nine still have not, and several states have passed legislation barring undocumented youth from enrolling in college. As this book was being written, the discourse on the citizenship of undocumented children of immigrants was growing more heated on both sides of the aisle. The DREAM Act is a controversial legislative proposal that would allow undocumented children of immigrants who arrived prior to age sixteen and who have completed high school or their GED the opportunity to apply for and attain citizenship if they meet certain other requirements. As we have demonstrated, given the opportunity and the preparation to do so, children of immigrants want to give back to their communities, and they do so with enthusiasm. Our substantive analyses were limited to those children of immigrants who were citizens at the time of the 2000 election (and the 2008 election in the case of our qualitative data); legislation such as the DREAM Act could not only greatly expand the civic participation but also permit the political participation of the undocumented children of immigrants. Despite their schooling and socialization in the U.S. educational system, this growing segment of the population transitions from adolescence to early adulthood with limited educational and professional opportunities, owing to circumstances beyond their control. Maximizing their civic and political potential could only strengthen U.S. civic society.

The Civic Role of Schools   What is perhaps the most interesting finding from our study is the estimated effect of the school social science curriculum, in particular its effect on early adult political behavior. Students who earn higher social science GPAs are more likely to participate in the political system through registering to vote and voting in young adulthood. Children of immigrants who take more social science coursework are similarly predisposed to political involvement compared to their peers who take fewer social science courses. Learning more about civic society and putting forth effort in the classes appears to encourage political participation, consistent with prior research linking civic knowledge obtained during adolescence to later political participation (Galston 2001; Youniss et al. 1997). Social science preparation, above and beyond math and science achievement and a general college preparatory curriculum, is associated with active political participation, suggesting that the high school civics curriculum will remain relevant even in an increasingly disconnected society (Putnam 2000).

The role of social science course-taking is especially important in light of the negligible association in our work between parental education level and the voting behaviors of children of immigrants. Whereas parental education level largely explains voting behaviors among children of native-born parents, it demonstrates little influence among children of immigrants. In lieu of parental experience with the political system, the social science curriculum appears to guide the civic development of these relatively new citizens. Although generation 1.5 is more likely to hold citizenship than their parents, second-generation immigrants are by definition citizens; both groups of students are schooled in the United States across a variety of states, districts, and schools. In an era of heightened attention to the subjects prioritized by state assessments, it is important to remember the function of schools that contributes to students' understanding of our democratic system—and ultimately the functioning of our democracy.

The Social Role of School   Our findings suggest that the community of the school can foster a positive political socialization of students. In addition to the courses taught in social science and other subjects, we found that students' sense of community within the high school is associated with their political behavior during young adulthood. Schools contribute to the socialization of the leaders of tomorrow not only through the civic discourse of the social science classroom but also through more informal experiences, such as extracurricular involvement, volunteering, and a sense of social connection among students. As we observed earlier, immigrant youth behave much like their third-plus-generation peers when it comes to the social connections they develop within and around school. Schools offer not only an academic foundation but also a template for social connection to formal institutions in our society that will remain with these young adults throughout their lifetimes.

For adolescents, high school provides a forum and a community in which they can forge an identity and knowledge base independent of their parents and families and begin to participate in our society and political system. American high schools present a venue in which immigrant youth can begin to assimilate into American society as they prepare for the transition into young adulthood. High schools provide adolescents with an early experience of belonging to a community outside the home and independent of it that can be formative in their development into active citizens.

Just as a connection to community is associated with adults' electoral engagement, we found that a student's connection to school is highly associated with future political participation. Students who reported feeling part of the school, feeling like they belonged, were more likely to be politically involved in young adulthood compared to their peers who felt less connected and, in some cases, more alone at school. Importantly, a higher level of connection in a school on average is also associated with the future voting behavior of individual students, independent of their own sense of connection. The community of the school as a whole appears to contribute to political socialization. As the level of social connection at the school increases, so does an individual student's likelihood of political activity during young adulthood. Net of strong background controls, the effect of the student's own social connection on future political participation is enhanced by the school climate.

It is possible that connection during adolescence to the school as a formal institution sets the stage for future civic connection. It is even possible that strong social connection during high school results in network-style relationships that endure into early adulthood and that these relationships encourage political involvement. Although determining the exact mechanism is beyond the scope of our work, our findings affirm the important role of high schools in preparing adolescents for civic involvement during young adulthood. Based on previous literature, we initially anticipated that children of immigrants' future political involvement might be related to the presence of other immigrants in the school, and that this association would arise from enhanced social connections, the provision of curriculum tailored to the unique academic and linguistic needs of immigrants, or the effects of a stronger identity with an enclave community. However, we found no evidence of such an association in our analyses. Instead, our evidence suggests the importance of a welcoming school environment in promoting the future political participation of immigrant youth and children of native-born parents alike.

Limitations to Our Study and Directions for Future Research

As with any large-scale inquiry, our results are only as strong as the available data. Although both the Education Longitudinal Study (ELS) and National Longitudinal Study of Adolescent Health (Add Health) data sets offer rich survey data of a sizable sample of first- and second-generation youth, our analyses were constrained by an inability to disaggregate by racial and ethnic status and several other key immigrant characteristics. The limited sample sizes compelled us to explore the political trajectories of immigrant youth combined into two categories: children born abroad and children born in the United States to an immigrant parent or parents. Whenever possible, we separated out the immigrant sample by race and ethnicity, but more often than not this resulted in inadequate cell sizes. Our models all control on these characteristics, but the processes experienced by any given group cannot be contrasted with those of another group. It is imperative that as we move forward in the field we disaggregate not only by race and ethnicity but also by length of time in U.S. schools and age upon entry. In addition, some of the participants we classified as children of immigrants had one immigrant parent and one native-born parent. In all of these cases where our population definition was less than ideal, we conducted sensitivity analyses to determine whether our definition was misleading and presented only results that we determined were robust. In future research, identifying a larger, more viable sample would permit analysis along these important subgroupings.

We should also note that our analyses focused on schools and schooling in part because we are limited in our ability to explore the political socialization that undoubtedly occurs within the family, around the dinner table. Considerable prior research has explored the roles of family and community in other aspects of immigrant youths' incorporation, but we still know little about the political socialization of children of immigrants within the family. To date, no large-scale data sets offer viable measures of immigrant parents' political knowledge and beliefs, nor do any measure the transmission of civic knowledge with a sufficient sample of immigrant parents and their children.

Our data are limited to broad measures of social science preparation such as credits completed and grades. Further research might explore the more nuanced ways in which this coursework in particular functions to shape political involvement. For example, which aspects of the curriculum or elements of teachers' pedagogy are particularly salient in shaping political participation among immigrant youth? Findings from our interviews with teachers and Latino immigrant young adults suggest that the discourse and expectations of these courses shape students' perspectives in young adulthood. As demonstrated in the content and discourse of high school social science coursework, the tools for future political voice and activity can be made available to immigrant youth.

However, the qualitative component of our study was purposefully limited in its focus on highly prepared, nationally board-certified teachers and the former students whom they suggested as study participants. It is likely that many if not most immigrant students—and especially immigrant, Latino, language minority youth—do not have the opportunity to enroll in courses taught by such high-caliber teachers. Future research exploring ways in which general and EL-certified social science teachers might bring out the strengths of children of immigrants would help shape our understanding of school processes for *all* immigrant youth developing their civic voices.

IMPLICATIONS FOR POLICY AND PRACTICE

How could educators and policymakers incorporate our findings into the school experiences of immigrant youth today? These stakeholders are concerned about not only their schools' effectiveness but also their relevance in an era of accountability. Even in a society dominated by a discourse of accountability, however, the importance of schools in developing citizens of the future should not be ignored. Schools contribute to students' political development through both promotion of a positive social climate and individual engagement in social science coursework. Policymakers interested in improving the effectiveness of their districts and local communities in producing politically involved young adults would do well to support strong social science programs.

In addition, the growing population of children of immigrants may be critical to the nation's political future. As one of the fastest-growing segments of the youth population, children of immigrants are poised to make a difference in the political future of the United States, as evidenced in the immigrant marches of 2006 and the upswing of the youth and minority vote in the 2008 and 2012 presidential elections. As we note, schools do not influence *how* children of immigrants vote, but rather *whether* they vote. The ability of schools to motivate children of immigrants' civic participation through social science coursework speaks to the untapped potential of this growing demographic.

In playing an important role in shaping the political behaviors of the growing immigrant young adult population, schools act as institutions of the state. Our findings point to the salience of social science content among immigrant youth. Local educational agencies vested in a sound civic future for their communities will want to take advantage of immigrant youths' connections to the social science content as one important way of ensuring that they have access to the full scope of civics coursework. This would involve a content-based approach for immigrant adolescents enrolled in ESL coursework—that is, shaping the development of these students' academic English proficiency through negotiation of political awareness and civic development.

Thoughts for the Future

A considerable literature has focused on the role of parents and the community in the social, academic, and professional incorporation of the growing population of children of immigrants. Our study addresses the unique role of the school, which, we argue, supplements the role of the family and the com-

munity in important ways. Schools provide the opportunities to learn prioritized by local administrators and teachers, within the parameters of state
graduation and college entrance requirements. These opportunities appear to
prepare students who are children of immigrants for political participation
and possibly for positions of leadership in their communities. It may be that
the curriculum provided by schools is a valuable resource that these students
deconstruct and negotiate within their families and communities and that
they apply their new knowledge in ways that best serve the needs of their
families and communities. With a clearer understanding of the role of schools
and schooling in relation to community and neighborhood, future inquiry
can begin to parse the familial and community-based aspects of the political
incorporation of this growing demographic subgroup.

Although youth voter turnout began to increase following the 2000 election (López et al. 2006; López, Marcelo, and Kirby 2007), there is substantial
room for improvement in turnout rates, especially among young adults who
are children of immigrants. While our findings suggest a strong relationship
between social science course-taking and the political involvement of young
adults, the fact remains that immigrant youth take significantly fewer social
science credits than do their third-plus-generation peers. As the children of
immigrants population grows, attention to their political socialization is imperative for our nation's future.

Improving access to opportunities to learn and succeed in school will not
only promote youths' overall academic preparation for the labor force and
higher education but also contribute to the health of our democracy. As was
the case in the early years of public schooling, this study suggests a key role
for schools in the political socialization of youth today. Beyond the contribution of schools to our nation's economic future, our work suggests that the
health of our nation's democracy hinges in part on the health of our schools.
Presumably, early adult voters will develop habits that continue throughout
their lifetimes. Our work suggests that investing in the education of children
of immigrants immediately before their transition to adulthood results in an
excellent return for our political system in the long run.

APPENDIX

Data and Methods

Our analyses drew on three distinct data sets in order to address our research questions. Here we explain the specifics of the three data sets and discuss their relevance to our study.

The National Longitudinal Study of Adolescent Health and the Adolescent Health and Academic Achievement Study

The National Longitudinal Study of Adolescent Health (Add Health) is a nationally representative longitudinal data set of over 20,000 students in a sample of eighty U.S. high schools, each with one feeder school sampled proportional to its representation of the high school's student body (Bearman, Jones, and Udry 1997; Harris and Udry 2011).[1] An in-school survey was administered to all students attending school in the spring of the 1994–1995 academic year. The survey sample was augmented using school records to draw a representative sample of boys and girls (in equal numbers) in grades seven to twelve to participate in the Add Health longitudinal study. We used the three waves of survey data that were collected in 1994–1995 (wave 1), 1996 (wave 2), and 2000–2001 (wave 3; the wave 3 sample includes 15,163 young adults).

In 2002–2003, when almost all Add Health respondents were no longer attending high school, the Adolescent Health and Academic Achievement Study (AHAA) collected high school transcripts and other education data from the last high school that wave 3 Add Health respondents attended (Muller et al. 2007). Transcripts were collected and coded for 12,250 wave 3 respondents—over 80 percent of the wave 3 sample. Each course that appeared on the transcript was coded with a standard coding scheme, the Classification System for Secondary Courses (CSSC), using information provided by the schools about course offerings. Grades were coded in a standard format, and the courses were assigned Carnegie Units (defined as 120 hours of coursework in a given subject) for comparability across schools. The AHAA study excluded two of the eighty high schools in the Add Health sample because they were special education schools and did not keep transcript records of students' courses.

In addition to the Add Health data, the yearbooks of selected Add Health base-year high schools were investigated by Chandra Muller as part of a planning study (funded by the William T. Grant Foundation). In chapter 3, we describe some of the findings from this study. Although the selected yearbooks were completely coded, including linking of students across extracurricular activities, they were not linked to the main Add Health database.

Most of our analyses drew on data from AHAA because the focus of our research is on the effects of academic and school experiences and outcomes. For these analyses, our sample included only the students who were in waves 1 and 3 and in the AHAA study. An exception is described in chapter 3, where our analysis of the social experiences of students (both children of immigrant and children of native-born parents) in high schools relies on a larger sample of students—those who were in wave 1. Weights were designed for the Add Health and AHAA studies to account for the complex sample design and nonresponse. All analyses were weighted.

For our purposes, the Add Health and AHAA data have several strengths. First, Add Health has a large sample of immigrants: 21.1 percent of the unweighted and 15.1 percent of the weighted AHAA sample members were born to one or more immigrant parents. Second, the Add Health questionnaire includes questions about whether young adult respondents were or had become U.S. citizens by the 2000 election, whether they voted, and whether they identified with a political party; we use this information in Chapter 6. And finally, Add Health has unusually large within-school samples and rich information about adolescents' relationships with their peers. For simplicity, we refer to Add Health to mean the combined Add Health and AHAA data.

Education Longitudinal Study: 2002 to 2006

The Education Longitudinal Study of 2002 (ELS), provides individual, family, and school characteristics of a nationally representative sample of sophomores enrolled during the 2001–2002 school year (Ingels et al. 2007).[2] Over 15,000 sophomores nested in about 750 public and private high schools were surveyed in the spring of 2002. Respondents were surveyed again in 2004 and 2006. In 2005 transcripts were collected from the high school last attended by these students. Through a procedure comparable to the one used in the AHAA study, transcripts were assigned CSSC codes.

With its rich information about academics and high schools for a large sample of sophomores, ELS provides excellent data about the academic achievement—including math and reading test scores—and course-taking patterns of this sophomore cohort. The math and reading achievement test scores provide valuable indicators of students' content knowledge and achievement in these basic subject areas. Along with the complete high school transcripts for more than 14,726 of these students, ELS provides a rich database for an examination of the processes that influence high school achievement and preparation for college.

For our purposes, however, ELS had several drawbacks. The information about students' immigrant status was available only in the parent questionnaire, and many parents (especially those who did not speak English) did not respond to the survey. In the ELS base year, information about immigrant status was missing for 14.1 percent of the students (13.8 percent unweighted). Of those with known immigrant status, 22.1 percent (26.3 percent unweighted) of base-year sample members were children of immigrants. Although the wave 3 questionnaire asked respondents about voter registration and voting in the 2004 presidential election, the ELS questionnaires did not ask respondents about citizenship status, which is critical for understanding voting among the first generation. For our purposes, the large sample of sophomores combined with the excellent test score data provided outstanding indicators of college preparation. We relied on ELS mainly to benchmark the academic experiences—especially course-taking and grades—of children of immigrants and children of native-born parents. These analyses appear in chapters 3 and 4.

The High Schools and Students in the Add Health and ELS Databases

Schools and their communities have a well-documented impact on students' academic and social experiences. Table A.1 shows some of the basic characteristics of the schools in each database. Although both databases are nationally representative of students, with only seventy-eight schools in the AHAA, the schools are not representative of high schools in the nation. The schools in the database are mostly comparable with respect to distribution across region of the country. ELS has more rural schools, and Add Health has a heavier concentration of urban and suburban schools. Add Health schools enroll a higher average percentage of students of color compared to ELS. On average, about one-third (35 percent) of the student body in Add Health schools have parents with a college degree or higher, compared to 41 percent for ELS schools. Of course, schools are often segregated with respect to race, ethnicity, and socioeconomic status, as is apparent in the large standard deviations for these averages.

Of the nearly 11 million immigrant youth in the U.S. school system in 2000, approximately 75 percent were native-born or second-generation; that is, one or more of their parents was an immigrant or foreign-born (Fix and Passel 2003). A rich body of literature has documented differences in both background characteristics and academic achievement outcomes of children of immigrants—both first- and second-generation—compared to the children of native-born parents (Bankston and Zhou 2002; Kao and Tienda

Table A.1   High School Characteristics

Variable	Add Health (N = 78)		ELS (N = 750)	
	Mean/ Proportion	Standard Deviation	Mean/ Proportion	Standard Deviation
West	0.20		0.19	
Northeast	0.19		0.17	
South	0.38		0.35	
Midwest	0.24		0.29	
Urban	0.30		0.21	
Suburban	0.53		0.42	
Rural	0.18		0.37	
Public	0.89		0.80	
Private	0.11		0.20	
Proportion of students				
Taking ESL	0.03	0.06		
Limited English proficient			0.04	0.08
Black	0.16	0.21	0.15	0.22
White	0.58	0.29	0.60	0.34
Latino	0.14	0.18	0.13	0.21
Asian	0.05	0.08	0.11	0.18
First-generation	0.08	0.10	0.10	0.14
Second-generation	0.09	0.10	0.15	0.17
Third-plus (non-immigrant)	0.83	0.19	0.74	0.27
Parents without high school diploma	0.10	0.12	0.06	0.10
Parents with college education	0.35	0.18	0.41	0.23
Student usually speaks language other than English at home	0.09	0.15		
Foreign-born: student's neighborhood	0.07	0.11		
Age five or older not speaking English well: student's neighborhood	0.03	0.06		
Linguistically isolated: student's neighborhood	0.03	0.06		

Source: Add Health (Bearman et al. 1997) and Education Longitudinal Study (Ingels et al. 2004).

1995; Portes and Rumbaut 2001; Rumbaut and Portes 2001). Children of immigrants differ from the children of native-born parents in their socioeconomic status and other factors that place them at higher risk and may threaten their educational success and overall development (Hernandez 2004). Our analyses further explore the association between educational experiences and civic outcomes for both children of immigrants and native-born parents.

Table A.2 shows the background characteristics of children of immigrants compared to the children of native-born parents, in both Add Health and ELS. Consistent with prior literature, children of immigrants were less likely to be white, and they came from homes with relatively lower levels of parental education. Children of immigrants were more likely to be racial or ethnic minorities, to have parents with lower levels of education, and to speak a language other than English at home. Their verbal and reading skills were, on average, lower than those of children of native-born parents, as indicated by their scores on the Picture Vocabulary Test (PVT) abbreviated by Add Health (AH-PVT) and the reading test administered to most ELS sophomores. For the most part, students in the two data sets were distributed similarly with respect to background.

Analytic Approaches and Key Variables

To understand the political socialization of adolescent children of immigrants as they transition to adulthood, we have relied on some of our previously published research combined with new analyses. When appropriate, we provide references to these articles to make more details of the analysis and variables available to the interested reader. In some cases, the models that we estimate here include slightly different variables, for internal consistency. However, in general our analytic approach is either described in this text or in the published article that we cite. In the remainder of this section, we describe some of the key variables that we use throughout this book.

CHILDREN OF IMMIGRANTS

We define children of immigrants as adolescents who have at least one parent born outside of the United States. In the Add Health data set, we use variables from the wave 1 in-home survey, which determined whether the student's place of birth, as well as that of each parent, was outside of the United States. If a student reported a birthplace outside of the United States, we coded that student as a first-generation immigrant. If a student reported being born in the United States and one or more of the parents reported a birthplace outside of the United States, we coded that student as a second-

Table A.2 Student Background Characteristics, by Generation

Variables	Add Health		ELS	
	Children of Immigrants (N = 2,445)	Children of Native-Born (N = 9,128)	Children of Immigrants (N = 3,281)	Children of Native-Born (N = 9,457)
Race				
White	0.23	0.74	0.21	0.73
Black	0.06	0.18	0.08	0.15
Asian	0.22	0.01	0.16	0.01
Filipino	0.07	0.00	0.04	0.00
Chinese	0.04	0.00	0.04	0.00
Asian Indian (South Indian)	0.01	0.00	0.03	0.00
Japanese	0.01	0.00	0.01	0.00
Korean	0.02	0.00	0.03	0.00
Vietnamese	0.03	0.00		
Southeast Asian			0.05	0.00
Other Asian	0.05	0.00		
Latino/a	0.45	0.05	0.49	0.06
Mexican	0.23	0.03	0.33	0.05
Cuban	0.04	0.00	0.02	0.00
Central/South American	0.07	0.00	0.08	0.00
Puerto Rican	0.04	0.01	0.05	0.01
Other Latino	0.03	0.00		
Gender				
Female	0.48	0.49	0.50	0.50
Language				
Non-native-English speaker	0.44	0.00	0.56	0.02
Parent education				
Less than high school	0.27	0.08	0.18	0.03
High school	0.26	0.38	0.18	0.20
Some college	0.16	0.20	0.29	0.38
College graduate or more	0.30	0.33	0.35	0.39
Academic indicators				
AH-PVT	97.11 (14.09)	103.15 (13.73)		
Reading test score			27.20 (9.16)	30.68 (9.99)
Math test score			35.35 (11.31)	38.50 (12.24)

Source: Add Health (Bearman et al. 1997) and Education Longitudinal Study (Ingels et al. 2004).
Note: Proportions and means; standard deviations in parentheses.

generation immigrant. Together, these two groups—first- and second-generation—make up the category of children of immigrants. We coded respondents born in the United States to U.S.-born parents as third-plus-generation, or children of native-born parents.

As mentioned earlier, in the ELS database parents' birthplace was available only from the parent questionnaire, which had a response rate of 87.4 percent of base-year students. Using the information in the parent questionnaire, we defined children of immigrants using the responses to three questions about the birthplaces of the student, the mother, and the father. We considered first whether the student was born in the United States (including Puerto Rico) or abroad; we coded foreign-born students as first-generation children of immigrants. Next, we considered whether either one of the student's parents was born outside of the United States; we coded those students with one or more foreign-born parents as second-generation children of immigrants. We coded student respondents who were born in the United States to U.S.-born parents as children of native-born parents.

COURSEWORK

The analyses in chapters 4 through 6 rely on students' high school course-taking data. In general, the construction of the specific variables is described elsewhere. Nonetheless, it is worth describing the transcript data—available for both the Add Health/AHAA and ELS samples—and their role in our analyses. Students' transcripts provide a rich and valuable record of their academic experiences throughout the high school years. Even when students are not surveyed the year they enter high school—the case for all ELS students and for the sophomore through senior cohorts of Add Health—their transcripts provide information about academic placement in their freshman year. Because opportunities to learn tend to be cumulative over the years of elementary, middle school, and high school, benchmarking students' positions in the academic hierarchy when they enter high school provides a valuable control for models that estimate the effects of other high school experiences on outcomes. We typically used students' math course placement for this purpose.

We also used students' transcripts to measure their exposure to social science courses and their performance in those classes (their grades). Our approach to defining a social science course is described in greater detail in our prior work using Add Health (Callahan et al. 2008). We also present ELS-based statistics in chapter 4 and use a similar approach, made possible by the fact that transcripts are coded using the same system in the two data sets. Once the CSSC codes for social science courses were defined, we could easily compute the grade point averages earned in those courses.

New Citizens in a New Century

Throughout the book, but especially in chapter 5, we introduce qualitative data from the New Citizens in a New Century study. Data collection was conducted by Rebecca Callahan and her graduate assistant, C. Allen Lynn. This supplemental qualitative study was designed to enrich the quantitative material and analyses that we developed for this study. In our initial quantitative analyses, we observed what seemed to be important differences in the responses of children of immigrants to their exposure to social science. Although we were able to document variation in the estimated effects of social science course-taking between immigrant and native-born youth, very little was known about actual social science teaching and experiences. We wanted to explore teachers' and immigrant students' perceptions of social science classes. In particular, we hoped to explore their perceptions of *how* the content of social science courses might contribute to political socialization. In addition, we found little, if any, movement in the political participation of Asian immigrant youth. The immigrant coefficient in our models was driven largely by Latino immigrant youth in our samples; Asian youth, regardless of generational status, simply did not vote at any significant rate. Ultimately, we chose to pursue a supplemental qualitative study designed to explore what it is that happens during high school social science coursework that teachers and students perceive as responsible for shaping later political participation.

Any qualitative sample identified to explore the social science experiences of immigrant Latino youth is likely to reflect the bifurcation in the academic experiences and exposure demonstrated by this group. Given our knowledge of nationally representative course-taking patterns among Latino immigrant youth, we knew that a random sampling of teachers and schools, even in high-Latino-immigrant communities, was likely to yield few students who had taken advanced social science courses. Our prior analysis suggested that immigrant youth who take more (read: advanced) social science coursework are more likely to vote. To capitalize on this trend, Rebecca Callahan identified and interviewed nationally board-certified high school social science teachers.

The decision to target nationally board-certified teachers was a conscious effort to highlight optimal pedagogical practices among a relatively underserved group of students, Latino/a children of immigrants. Board certification not only provides a measure of peer recognition in the field but also verifies that a teacher has undergone a rigorous application and certification process to confirm his or her exemplary status as a curricular and pedagogical expert in a particular content area. Prior research indicates that students of board-certified teachers have significantly higher levels of academic achievement compared to students of non-board-certified teachers (Goldhaber and Anthony 2007; Vandevoort and Berliner 2004). For the purposes of the pres-

Table A.3   Nationally Board-Certified Teacher Participants

Pseudonym	Region of Residence	Social Science Courses Taught	Ethnicity
Mr. Gordon	Chicago	U.S. and world history, Latin American studies	White
Ms. Foster	New York	Government	White
Ms. Jewel	Chicago	Government, civics, law	White
Mr. Jones	Florida	U.S. history	White
Ms. McDougal	Chicago	U.S history, world studies	White
Ms. Martínez	Texas	World history, European history	Latina
Mr. Rocca	Florida	European history	White
Mr. Schroeder	San Diego	World history	White
Mr. Tomasi	San Diego	World history	White

Source: New Citizens in a New Century (Callahan 2008).

ent study, national board certification offered a tangible measure of teachers' pedagogical and curricular expertise, which was likely to have a positive impact on their students' future political engagement.

Specifically, we approached nationally board-certified high school social science teachers in five high-Latino, high-immigrant communities in San Diego, Chicago, New York, Texas, and Florida. We contacted teachers working with children of immigrants in high-Latino schools in each of the regions. In all, we interviewed thirteen nationally board-certified high school social science teachers in one- to two-hour-long, semistructured interviews. Table A.3 shows the characteristics of the nine teachers whose data contributed to this book. An unintended consequence of their selection was an opportunity to explore honors social science courses, because our teachers taught these courses, as shown in the table. More importantly, however, our sample teachers all taught Latino children of immigrants, many of whom were also economically disadvantaged. Throughout their interviews, participating teachers reflected on the intersection of language, ethnicity, and social class in their classrooms and offered a rich view of the academic lives of the children of immigrants.

The interview protocols addressed, but were not limited to, issues of curriculum, pedagogical practices, in-class and out-of-class activities, service learning opportunities, teacher-student relationships, and immigrant youth political participation. During the interviews, participants were asked to expand on the social and academic processes in the high school social science context that they thought might contribute to encouraging students to vote when they became eligible.

Before interviewing the teachers, we asked them to identify former stu-

Table A.4   Latino/a Immigrant Young Adult Participants

Pseudonym	Gender	Age	Generation	State of Residence	Ethnicity
Amanda	F	21	Second	Texas	Mexican
Anthony	M	24	First	Texas	Mexican
Fatima	F	20	Second	California	Mexican
Fernando	M	21	Second	Texas	Argentinean-Guatemalan
Genaro	M	24	Second	New York	Cuban-Dominican
Isabel	F	20	Second	California	Mexican
Juan	M	20	First	Florida	Colombian
Ramiro	M	20	Second	Florida	Cuban
Rosita	F	20	Second	Florida	Mexican
Sam	M	21	First	Texas	Mexican

Source: New Citizens in a New Century (Callahan 2008).

dents who were Latino children of immigrants and would have been eligible to vote in the 2008 election for participation in the study. The teachers then contacted their former students on our behalf to gain permission for us to make contact and request an interview. The young adult sample was limited to Latinos because our previous research indicated that social science course-taking has an effect on voting for Latino immigrants but not for Asian immigrants (Callahan et al. 2008). For this study, Rebecca Callahan and her graduate assistant, C. Allen Lynn, interviewed a total of seventeen former students between the ages of eighteen and twenty-four during one- to two-hour-long, semistructured interviews. Table A.4 lists the Latino/a immigrant young adults whose voices are heard in this book.

In our interviews with the former Latino immigrant students, now young adults, we explored their perceptions of their high school social science experiences. In addition, Rebecca Callahan asked the participants to expand on the development of their civic and political identities in young adulthood. Focused on civic and political coming of age, interviews with the young adult participants explored a range of experiences that may have shaped their civic and political integration in young adulthood.

NOTES

Introduction

1. To protect the privacy of our interviewees, all names used here are pseudonyms.
2. The education of immigrant youth, the majority of whom speak a language other than English, is governed by two key legal decisions asserting students' right to an education. The first (Lau) established the right to an education through support while learning English. The second (Castañeda) clarified that the language support programs established under Lau needed to be (1) based on sound educational research and theory, (2) be instructionally sound, and (3) evaluated to ensure student growth. Lau v. Nichols, 414 U.S. 563 (9th Dist. 1974); Castañeda v. Pickard, 648 F.2d 989 (5th Cir., Unit A, 1981).

Chapter 1

1. We do not include black children of immigrants and Asian children of natives in figure 1.6 because, in some of the survey years, the Current Population Survey Voting and Registration Supplements contained insufficient numbers of cases for these groups to produce reliable estimates

Chapter 2

1. The federal term for language minority students learning English is "limited English proficient" (LEP), but many states and local education agencies (LEAs) use the term "English language learner" (ELL) instead. For the purposes of this study, and to bypass a deficit perspective, we use the term ELL to refer to a language minority student designated by the school to be in the process of learning English.

Chapter 3

1. We explored differences in these trends by whether the student was a first- or second-generation immigrant and found no significant differences between the two groups.
2. Much attention in the literature has been devoted to the relative effects of schools and neighborhoods on the development of children (see, for example, Leventhal and Brooks-Gunn 2000). Although such an investigation is beyond the scope of our research, it is worth noting that schools and neighborhoods are both affected by socioeconomic resources. Notably, school composition and resources, to the extent that they are a function of the families and communities served by the school, have effects that are difficult to assign to either school or neighborhood.

Chapter 4

1. For a historical overview of the educational policy that has shaped the schooling of language minority immigrant students, see Hakuta (2011).

Chapter 5

1. We would like to thank Dr. Cawo Abdi for the connections she made across our research. Dr. Abdi suggests that immigrant parents' preparation for the civics component of the U.S. citizenship test is a mechanism through which their children's social science coursework on citizenship becomes more salient for them. In her own work with Somali families, Dr. Abdi has found that many families prominently display the parents' citizenship brochure and study guides.

Chapter 6

1. In table 6.2, students who were registered to vote as young adults are contrasted with those who were not registered. In models not shown, we used multinomial regression to estimate coefficients for three categories of early adult voters: those who did not register, those who registered but did not vote, and those who voted. Substantively, our conclusions are similar, and we present results from the logistic regressions for simplicity and ease of interpretation. We mention a few instances where our conclusions would be modified had we presented the multinomial regression coefficients.
2. This effect is not significant in multinomial models when those who registered to vote but did not vote are distinguished from those who voted.

Appendix

1. For online information on the Add Health data set, see: http://www.icpsr.umich.edu/icpsrweb/ICPSR/studies/21600. Accessed December 31, 2012.
2. For online information on the ELS data set, see: http://nces.ed.gov/surveys/els2002. Accessed December 31, 2012.

REFERENCES

Adelman, Clifford. 1999. *Answers in the Tool Box: Academic Intensity, Attendance Patterns, and Bachelor's Degree Attainment.* Washington: U.S. Department of Education, Office of Educational Research and Improvement.

———. 2004. *Principal Indicators of Student Academic Histories in Postsecondary Education, 1972–2000.* Washington: U.S. Department of Education, Institute of Education Sciences.

———. 2006. "The Toolbox Revisited: Paths to Degree Completion from High School Through College." Washington: U.S. Department of Education.

Akerlof, George A., and Rachel E. Kranton. 2002. "Identity and Schooling: Some Lessons for the Economics of Education." *Journal of Economic Literature* 40(4): 1167–1201.

Alba, Richard D., and Victor Nee. 1997. "Rethinking Assimilation Theory for a New Era of Immigration." *International Migration Review* 31(4): 826–74.

Anyon, Jean. 1988. "Schools as Agencies of Social Legitimation." In *Contemporary Curriculum Discourses,* edited by William F. Pinar. Scottsdale, Ariz.: Gorsuch Scarisbrick.

Arbona, Consuelo, and Amaury Nora. 2007. "The Influence of Academic and Environmental Factors on Hispanic College Degree Attainment." *Review of Higher Education* 30(3): 247–69.

Atherton, Herbert M. 2000. "We the People . . . Project Citizen." In *Education for Civic Engagement in Democracy: Service Learning and Other Promising Practices,* edited by Sheilah Mann and John J. Patrick. Bloomington, Ind.: ERIC Clearinghouse for Social Studies/Social Science Education.

Atkins, Robert, and Daniel Hart. 2003. "Neighborhoods, Adults, and the Development of Civic Identity in Urban Youth." *Applied Developmental Science* 7(3): 156–64.

Azmitia, Margarita, and Catherine R. Cooper. 2001. "Good or Bad? Peer Influences on Latino and European American Adolescents' Pathways Through School." *Journal of Education for Students Placed at Risk* 6(1,2): 45–71.

Bailey, Gahan, Edward L. Shaw Jr., and Donna Hollifield. 2006. "The Devaluation of Social Studies in the Elementary Grades." *Journal of Social Studies Research* 30(2): 18–29.

Bankston, Carl L., and Min Zhou. 1995. "Effects of Minority-Language Literacy on the Academic Achievement of Vietnamese Youths in New Orleans." *Sociology of Education* 68(1): 1–17.

———. 1997. "The Social Adjustment of Vietnamese American Adolescents: Evidence for a Segmented Assimilation Approach." *Social Science Quarterly* 78(2): 508–23.

———. 2002. "Social Capital and Immigrant Children's Achievement." In *Schooling and Social Capital in Diverse Cultures,* vol. 13, *Research in Sociology of Education,* edited by Bruce Fuller and Emily Hannum. Bingley, U.K.: Emerald.

Bearman, Peter S., Jo Jones, and J. Richard Udry. 1997. *The National Longitudinal Study of Adolescent Health: Research Design.* Chapel Hill: University of North Carolina, Carolina Population Center.

Bloemraad, Irene, and Christine Trost. 2008. "It's a Family Affair." *American Behavioral Scientist* 52(4): 507–32.

Brady, Henry E., Sidney Verba, and Kay L. Schlozman. 1995. "Beyond SES: A Resource Model of Political Participation." *American Political Science Review* 89(2): 271–94.

Bratsberg, Bernt, and James F. Ragan Jr. 2002. "The Impact of Host-Country Schooling on Earnings: A Study of Male Immigrants in the United States." *Journal of Human Resources* 37(1): 63–105.

Broh, Beckett A. 2002. "Linking Extracurricular Programming to Academic Achievement: Who Benefits and Why?" *Sociology of Education* 75(1): 69–91.

Burroughs, Susie, Eric Groce, and Mary Lee Webeck. 2005. "Social Studies Education in the Age of Testing and Accountability." *Educational Measurement: Issues and Practice* 24(3): 13–20.

Callahan, Rebecca M. 2005. "Tracking and High School English Learners: Limiting Opportunity to Learn." *American Educational Research Journal* 42(2): 305–28.

Callahan, Rebecca M., and Patricia C. Gándara. 2004. "On Nobody's Agenda: Improving English Language Learners' Access to Higher Education." In *Immigrant and Second Language Students: Lessons from Research and Best Practice,* edited by Michael Sadowski. Cambridge, Mass.: Harvard Education Press.

Callahan, Rebecca M., Chandra Muller, and Kathryn S. Schiller. 2008. "Preparing for Citizenship: Immigrant High School Students' Curriculum and Socialization." *Theory and Research in Social Education* 36(2): 6–31.

Callahan, Rebecca M., and Dara Shifrer. 2012. "High School ESL Placement: Practice, Policy, and Effects on Achievement." In *Linguistic Minority Students Go to College: Preparation, Access, and Persistence,* edited by Yasuko Kanno and Linda Harklau. New York: Routledge.

Callahan, Rebecca M., Lindsey Wilkinson, and Chandra Muller. 2010. "Academic Achievement and Course-Taking Among Language Minority Youth in U.S.

Schools: Effects of ESL Placement." *Educational Evaluation and Policy Analysis* 32(1): 84–117.

Callahan, Rebecca M., Lindsey Wilkinson, Chandra Muller, and Michelle L. Frisco. 2009. "ESL Placement and Schools: Effects on Immigrant Achievement." *Educational Policy* 23(2): 355–84.

Capps, Randolph, Michael Fix, Jason Ost, Jane Reardon-Anderson, and Jeffrey S. Passel. 2004. "The Health and Well-being of Young Children of Immigrants." Washington, D.C.: Urban Institute.

Capps, Randolph, Julie Murray, Jason Ost, Jeffrey S. Passel, and Shinta Herwantoro. 2005. *The New Demography of America's Schools: Immigration and the No Child Left Behind Act.* Washington, D.C.: Urban Institute.

Center for Information and Research on Civic Learning and Engagement (CIRCLE). 2011. "The Youth Vote in 2010: Final Estimates Based on Census Data." College Park: University of Maryland, School of Public Policy, CIRCLE.

Chaffee, Steven. 2000. "Education for Citizenship: Promising Effects of the Kids' Voting Curriculum." In *Education for Civic Engagement in Democracy: Service Learning and Other Promising Practices,* edited by Sheilah Mann and John J. Patrick. Bloomington, Ind.: ERIC Clearinghouse for Social Studies/Social Science Education.

Charmaz, Kathy. 2006. *Constructing Grounded Theory: A Practical Guide Through Qualitative Analysis.* Thousand Oaks, Calif.: Sage Publications.

Chaudry, Ajay, and Karina Fortuny. 2010. "Children of Immigrants: Family and Parental Characteristics." Brief 2. Washinton, D.C.: Urban Institute.

Cho, Wendy K. Tam. 1999. "Naturalization, Socialization, Participation: Immigrants and (Non-) Voting." *Journal of Politics* 61(4): 1140–55.

Cloonan, Martin, and John Street. 1998. "Rock the Vote: Popular Culture and Politics." *Politics* 18(1): 33–38.

Coleman, James S. 1990. *Foundations of Social Theory.* Cambridge, Mass.: Belknap Press of Harvard University Press.

Cooper, Catherine R., Robert G. Cooper, Margarita Azmitia, Gabriela Chavira, and Yvette Gullatt. 2002. "Bridging Multiple Worlds: How African American and Latino Youth in Academic Outreach Programs Navigate Math Pathways to College." *Applied Developmental Science* 6(2): 73–87.

Cortes, Kalena E. 2006. "The Effects of Age at Arrival and Enclave Schools on the Academic Performance of Immigrant Children." *Economics of Education Review* 25(2): 121–32.

Cosentino de Cohen, Clemencia, Nicole Deterding, and Beatriz Chu Clewell. 2005. "Who's Left Behind? Immigrant Children in High- and Low-LEP Schools." Washington, D.C.: Urban Institute.

Cremin, Lawrence A. 1951. *The American Common School: An Historic Conception.* New York: Teachers College Press.

Crosnoe, Robert, and Aletha C. Huston. 2007. "Socioeconomic Status, Schooling, and the Developmental Trajectories of Adolescents." *Developmental Psychology* 43(5): 1097–1110.

De Gaetano, Yvonne. 2007. "The Role of Culture in Engaging Latino Parents' Involvement in School." *Urban Education* 42(2): 145–62.

Delli Carpini, Michael X. 2000. "Gen.com: Youth, Civic Engagement, and the New Information Environment." *Political Communication* 17(4): 341–49.

Delli Carpini, Michael X., and Scott Keeter. 1997. *What Americans Know About Politics and Why It Matters.* New Haven, Conn.: Yale University Press.

Deschenes, Sarah, Larry Cuban, and David B. Tyack. 2001. "Mismatch: Historical Perspectives on Schools and Students Who Don't Fit Them." *Teachers College Record* 103(4): 525–47.

DeSipio, Louis. 2001. "Building America, One Person at a Time: Naturalization and Political Behavior of the Naturalized in Contemporary American Politics." In *E Pluribus Unum? Contemporary and Historical Perspectives on Immigrant Political Incorporation,* edited by Gary Gerstle and John H. Mollenkopf. New York: Russell Sage Foundation.

———. 2002. *Immigrant Organizing, Civic Outcomes: Civic Engagement, Political Activity, National Attachment, and Identity in Latino Immigrant Communities.* Irvine: University of California, Center for the Study of Democracy.

Dondero, Molly, and Chandra Muller. 2012. "School Stratification in New and Established Latino Destinations." *Social Forces* 91(2): 477–502.

Downs, Anthony. 1957. "An Economic Theory of Political Action in a Democracy." *Journal of Political Economy* 65(2): 135–50.

Dronkers, Jaap, and Mark Levels. 2007. "Do School Segregation and School Resources Explain Region-of-Origin Differences in the Mathematics Achievement of Immigrant Students?" *Educational Research and Evaluation* 13(5): 435–62.

Dudley, Robert L., and Alan R. Gitelson. 2002. "Civic Education and Civic Engagement: A Return to Political Socialization?" *Applied Developmental Science* 6(4): 175–82.

Durand, Jorge, Edward Telles, and Jennifer Flashman. 2006. "The Demographic Foundations of the Latino Population." In *Hispanics and the Future of America,* edited by Marta Tienda and Faith Mitchell. Washington, D.C: National Academies Press.

Duursma, Elisabeth, Silvia Romero-Contreras, Anna Szuber, Patrick Proctor, Catherine Snow, Diane August, and Margarita Calderon. 2007. "The Role of Home Literacy and Language Environment on Bilinguals' English and Spanish Vocabulary Development." *Applied Psycholinguistics* 28(1): 171–90.

Eccles, Jacquelynne, and Bonnie Barber. 1999. "Student Council, Volunteering, Basketball, or Marching Band: What Kind of Extracurricular Involvement Matters?" *Journal of Adolescent Research* 14(1): 10–43.

Eccles, Jacquelynne S., Bonnie L. Barber, Margaret Stone, and James Hunt. 2003. "Extracurricular Activities and Adolescent Development." *Journal of Social Issues* 59(4): 865–89.

Fallace, Thomas D. 2008. "Did the Social Studies Really Replace History in American Secondary Schools?" *Teachers College Record* 110(10): 2245–70.

Faltis, Christian J., and Paula Wolfe. 1999. "So Much to Say: Adolescents, Bilingualism, and ESL in the Secondary School." New York: Teachers College Press.

Farkas, George. 1996. *Human Capital or Cultural Capital? Ethnicity and Poverty Groups in an Urban School District.* Hawthorne, N.Y.: Aldine de Gruyter.

Feliciano, Cynthia. 2005. "Does Selective Migration Matter? Explaining Ethnic Disparities in Educational Attainment Among Immigrants' Children." *International Migration Review* 39(4): 841–71.

Fix, Michael, and Jeffrey S. Passel. 2003. "U.S. Immigration: Trends and Implications for Schools." Washington, D.C.: Urban Institute.

Flanagan, Constance A., and Nakesha Faison. 2001. "Youth Civic Development: Implications for Research for Social Policy Programs." *Social Policy Report* 25(1): 1–16.

Fletcher, Anne C., Glen H. Elder Jr., and Debra Mekos. 2000. "Parental Influences on Adolescent Involvement in Community Activities." *Journal of Research on Adolescence* 10(1): 29–48.

Flynn, Nora K. 2009. "Toward Democratic Discourse: Scaffolding Student-Led Discussions in the Social Studies." *Teachers College Record* 111(8): 2021–54.

Fortuny, Karina. 2010. "Children of Immigrants: 2008 State Trends Update." Brief 17. Washington, D.C.: Urban Institute.

Frank, Kenneth, Chandra Muller, Kathryn Schiller, Catherine Riegle-Crumb, Anna Strassmann Mueller, Robert Crosnoe, and Jennifer Pearson. 2008. "The Social Dynamics of Mathematics Coursetaking in High School." *American Journal of Sociology* 113(6): 1645–96.

Fredricks, Jennifer A., and Jacquelynne S. Eccles. 2006. "Is Extracurricular Participation Associated with Beneficial Outcomes? Concurrent and Longitudinal Relations." *Developmental Psychology* 42(4): 698–713.

Freeman, Yvonne S., David E. Freeman, and Sandra Mercuri. 2002. *Closing the Achievement Gap: How to Reach Limited-Formal-Schooling and Long-Term English Learners.* Portsmouth, N.H.: Heinemann.

Frisco, Michelle L., Chandra Muller, and Kyle Dodson. 2004. "Participation in Voluntary Youth-Serving Associations and Early Adult Voting Behavior." *Social Science Quarterly* 85(3): 660–76.

Fry, Richard. 2002. *Latinos in Higher Education: Many Enroll, Too Few Graduate.* Washington, D.C.: Pew Hispanic Center.

———. 2006. *The Changing Landscape of American Schools: New Students, New Schools.* Washington, D.C.: Pew Hispanic Center.

Fuller, Bruce, and Emily Hannum. 2002. *Schooling and Social Capital in Diverse Cultures.* Amsterdam: JAI.

Galston, William A. 2001. "Political Knowledge, Political Engagement, and Civic Education." *Annual Review of Political Science* 4: 217–34.

Gamoran, Adam. 1987. "The Stratification of High School Learning Opportunities." *Sociology of Education* 60(3): 135–55.

———. 1992. "The Variable Effects of High School Tracking." *American Sociological Review* 57(6): 812–28.

———. 2001. "American Schooling and Educational Inequality: A Forecast for the Twenty-First Century." *Sociology of Education* 74: 135–53.

Gamoran, Adam, and Eileen C. Hannigan. 2000. "Algebra for Everyone? Benefits of College-Preparatory Mathematics for Students with Diverse Abilities in Early Secondary School." *Educational Evaluation and Policy Analysis* 22(3): 241–54.

Garet, Michael S., and Brian DeLany. 1988. "Students, Courses, and Stratification." *Sociology of Education* 61(2): 61–77.

Gimpel, James G., J. Celeste Lay, and Jason E. Schuknecht. 2003. *Cultivating Democracy: Civic Environments and Political Socialization in America.* Washington, D.C.: Brookings Institution Press.

Giordano, Peggy C. 2003. "Relationships in Adolescence." *Annual Review of Sociology* 29: 257–81.

Glanville, Jennifer L. 1999. "Political Socialization or Selection? Adolescent Extracurricular Participation and Political Activity in Early Adulthood." *Social Science Quarterly* 80(2): 279–90.

Glick, Jennifer E., and Michael J. White. 2003. "The Academic Trajectories of Immigrant Youths: Analysis Within and Across Cohorts." *Demography* 40(4): 759–83.

Golash-Boza, Tanya. 2005. "Assessing the Advantages of Bilingualism for the Children of Immigrants." *International Migration Review* 39(3): 721–53.

Goldhaber, Dan, and Emily Anthony. 2007. "Can Teacher Quality Be Effectively Assessed? National Board Certification as a Signal of Effective Teaching." *Review of Economics and Statistics* 89(1): 134–50.

Goodlad, John I. 1984. *A Place Called School.* New York: McGraw-Hill.

Green, Gillian, Jean Rhodes, Abigail Heitler Hirsch, Carola Suárez-Orozco, and Paul M. Camic. 2008. "Supportive Adult Relationships and the Academic Engagement of Latin American Immigrant Youth." *Journal of School Psychology* 46(4): 393–412.

Greer, Colin. 1969. "Public Schools: The Myth of the Melting Pot." In *Issues in Urban Education,* vol. 1, edited by Earl J. Ogletree. New York: MSS Information Corporation.

Grey, Anne C. 2009. "No Child Left Behind in Art Education Policy: A Review of Key Recommendations for Arts Language Revisions." *Arts Education Policy Review* 111(1): 8–15.

Guest, Andrew, and Barbara Schneider. 2003. "Adolescents' Extracurricular Participation in Context: The Mediating Effects of Schools, Communities, and Identity." *Sociology of Education* 76(2): 89–109.

Hagy, Alison P., and J. Farley Ordovensky Staniec. 2002. "Immigrant Status, Race, and Institutional Choice in Higher Education." *Economics of Education Review* 21(4): 381–92.

Hajnal, Zoltan L., and Taeku Lee. 2011. *Why Americans Don't Join the Party: Race, Immigration, and the Failure (of Political Parties) to Engage the Electorate.* Princeton, N.J.: Princeton University Press.

Hakuta, Kenji. 2011. "Educating Language Minority Students and Affirming Their Equal Rights." *Educational Researcher* 40(4): 163–74.

Hamann, Edmund T. 2008. "Meeting the Needs of ELLs: Acknowledging the Schism Between ESL/Bilingual and Mainstream Teachers and Illustrating That Problem's Remedy." In *Inclusive Pedagogy for English Language Learners: A Handbook of Research-Informed Practices,* edited by Lorrie Stoops Verplaetse and Naomi Migliacci. New York: Lawrence Erlbaum Associates.

Hanks, Michael. 1981. "Youth, Voluntary Associations and Political Socialization." *Social Forces* 60(1): 211–23.

Hao, Lingxin, and Melissa Bonstead-Bruns. 1998. "Parent-Child Differences in Educational Expectations and the Academic Achievement of Immigrant and Native Students." *Sociology of Education* 71(3): 175–98.

Hao, Lingxin, and Suet-ling Pong. 2008. "The Role of School in the Upward Mobility of Disadvantaged Immigrants' Children." *Annals of the American Academy of Political and Social Science* 620(1): 62–89.

Harker, Kathryn. 2001. "Immigrant Generation, Assimilation, and Adolescent Psychological Well-being." *Social Forces* 79(3): 969–1004.

Harklau, Linda. 1994a. "Jumping Tracks: How Language-Minority Students Negotiate Evaluations of Ability." *Anthropology and Education Quarterly* 25(3): 347–63.

———. 1994b. "Tracking and Linguistic Minority Students: Consequences of Ability Grouping for Second Language Learners." *Linguistics and Education* 6(3): 217–44.

Harris, Kathleen Mullan, and J. Richard Udry. 2011. "National Longitudinal Study of Adolescent Health (Add Health), 1994–2008." Ann Arbor: University of Michigan, Inter-university Consortium for Political and Social Research (ICPSR).

Hart, Daniel, Thomas M. Donnelly, James Youniss, and Robert Atkins. 2007. "High School Community Service as a Predictor of Adult Voting and Volunteering." *American Educational Research Journal* 44(1): 197–219.

Hernandez, Donald J. 2004. "Demographic Change and the Life Circumstances of Immigrant Families." *The Future of Children* 14(2): 17–47.

Hopstock, Paul J., and Todd G. Stephenson. 2003. "Descriptive Study of Services to LEP Students and LEP Students with Disabilities: Special Topic Report 1: Native Languages of LEP Students." Washington: U.S. Department of Education, Office of English Language Acquisition.

Hornberger, Nancy. 2006. "Frameworks and Models in Language Policy and Planning." In *An Introduction to Language Policy: Theory and Method,* edited by Thomas Ricento. Malden, Mass.: Blackwell Publishing.

Humphries, Melissa, Chandra Muller, and Kathryn S. Schiller. Forthcoming. "The Political Socialization of Children of Immigrants." *Social Science Quarterly.*

Huntington, Samuel. 2004. *Who Are We? The Challenges to America's National Identity.* New York: Simon & Schuster.

Huss-Keeler, Rebecca L. 1997. "Teacher Perception of Ethnic and Linguistic Minority Parental Involvement and Its Relationships to Children's Language and Literacy Learning: A Case Study." *Teaching and Teacher Education* 13(2): 171–82.

Ingels, Steven J., Thomas R. Curtin, Phillip Kaufman, Martha Naomi Alt, and Xianglei Chen. 2002. "Coming of Age in the 1990s: The Eighth Grade Class of 1988 Twelve Years Later: Initial Results from the Fourth Follow-up to the National Education Longitudinal Study of 1988." NCES 2002-321 (March). Washington: U.S. Department of Education, National Center for Education Statistics. Available at: http://nces.ed.gov/pubs2002/2002321.pdf. Accessed December 31, 2012.

Ingels, Steven J., Daniel J. Pratt, James E. Rogers, Peter H. Siegel, and Ellen S. Stutts. 2004. *Education Longitudinal Study of 2002: Base Year Data File User's Manual,* vol. NCES 2004.405. Washington, D.C.: U.S. Department of Education, National Center for Education Statistics.

Ingels, Steven J., Daniel J. Pratt, David Wilson, Laura J. Burns, Douglas Currivan, James E. Rogers, and Sherry Hubbard-Bednasz. 2007. *Educational Longitudinal Study of 2002: Base-Year to Second Follow-up Data File Documentation.* NCES 2008-347. Washington, D.C.: U.S. Department of Education, National Center for Education Statistics.

Jamieson, Amie, Hyon B. Shin, and Jennifer Day. 2002. *Voting and Registration in the Election of November 2000.* Washington: U.S. Bureau of the Census.

Jenness, David. 1990. *Making Sense of Social Studies:* New York: Macmillan.

Jennings, Jack, and Diane Stark Renter. 2006. "Ten Big Effects of the No Child Left Behind Act on Public Schools." *Phi Delta Kappan* 88(2): 110–13.

Jennings, M. Kent, and Richard G. Niemi. 1968. "The Transmission of Political Values from Parent to Child." *American Political Science Review* 62(1): 169–84.

Jennings, M. Kent, Laura Stoker, and Jake Bowers. 2009. "Politics Across Generations: Family Transmission Reexamined." *Journal of Politics* 71(3): 782–99.

Johnson, Martin, Robert M. Stein, and Robert Wrinkle. 2003. "Language Choice, Residential Stability, and Voting Among Latino Americans." *Social Science Quarterly* 84(2): 412–24.

Junn, Jane. 1999. "Participation in Liberal Democracy: The Political Assimilation of Immigrants and Ethnic Minorities in the United States." *American Behavioral Scientist* 42(9): 1417–38.

Kahne, Joseph, Bernadette Chi, and Ellen Middaugh. 2006. "Building Social Capital for Civic and Political Engagement: The Potential of High-School Civics Courses." *Canadian Journal of Education* 29(2): 387–409.

Kalogrides, Demetra. 2009. "Generational Status and Academic Achievement Among Latino High School Students: Evaluating the Segmented Assimilation Theory." *Sociological Perspectives* 52(2): 159–83.

Kao, Grace, and Jennifer S. Thompson. 2003. "Racial and Ethnic Stratification in

Educational Achievement and Attainment." *Annual Review of Sociology* 29: 417–42.

Kao, Grace, and Marta Tienda. 1995. "Optimism and Achievement: The Educational Performance of Immigrant Youth." *Social Science Quarterly* 76(1): 1–19.

Katz, Susan Roberta. 1999. "Teaching in Tensions: Latino Immigrant Youth, Their Teachers, and the Structures of Schooling." *Teachers College Record* 100(4): 809–40.

Kasinitz, Philip, John H. Mollenkopf, Mary C. Waters, and Jennifer Holdaway. 2009. *Inheriting the City: The Children of Immigrants Come of Age.* New York: Russell Sage Foundation.

Keeter, Scott, Molly Andolina, and Krista Jenkins. 2002. "The Civic and Political Health of the Nation: A Generational Portrait." New Brunswick, N.J.: CIRCLE and the Pew Charitable Trusts.

Keeter, Scott, Juliana Menasce Horowitz, and Alec Tyson. 2008. "Gen Dems: The Party's Advantage Among Young Voters Widens." Washington, D.C.: Pew Research Center.

Keller, Ursula, and Kathryn Harker Tillman. 2008. "Postsecondary Educational Attainment of Immigrant and Native Youth." *Social Forces* 87(1): 121–52.

Kelley, Jonathan, and Nan Dirk De Graaf. 1997. "National Context, Parental Socialization, and Religious Belief: Results from Fifteen Nations." *American Sociological Review* 62(4): 639–59.

Kirby, Emily Hoban, and Kei Kawashima-Ginsberg. 2009. "The Youth Vote in 2008." Medford, Mass.: Center for Information and Research on Civic Learning and Engagement.

Kloss, Heinz. 1977. *The American Bilingual Tradition.* Rowley, Mass.: Newbury House Publishers.

Leal, David L. 2002. "Political Participation by Latino Non-Citizens in the United States." *British Journal of Political Science* 32(2): 353–70.

Leming, Robert S. 1996. "We the People . . . The Citizen and the Constitution." Bloomington, Ind.: ERIC Clearinghouse for Social Studies/Social Science Education.

Leventhal, Tama, and Jeanne Brooks-Gunn. 2000. "The Neighborhoods They Live In: The Effects of Neighborhood Residence on Child and Adolescent Outcomes." *Psychological Bulletin* 126(2): 309–37.

Levine, Peter. 2007. *The Future of Democracy: Developing the Next Generation of American Citizens.* Medford, Mass.: Tufts University Press.

Levitt, Peggy. 2002. "Two Nations Under God? Latino Religious Life in the United States." In *Latinos: Remaking America,* edited by Marcelo M. Suárez-Orozco and Mariela M. Páez. Berkeley: University of California Press.

Levstik, Linda S., and Keith C. Barton. 2001. "Committing Acts of History: Mediated Action, Humanistic Education, and Participatory Democracy." In *Critical Issues in Social Studies Research for the Twenty-First Century,* edited by William B. Stanley. Greenwich, Conn.: Information Age Publishing.

Linquanti, Robert. 2001. "The Redesignation Dilemma: Challenges and Choices in Fostering Meaningful Accountability for English Learners." University of California Linguistic Minority Research Institute, WestEd.

López, Mark Hugo, Emily Kirby, and Jared Sagoff. 2005. *The Youth Vote 2004*. College Park, Md.: University of Maryland, School of Public Policy, Center for Information and Research on Civic Learning and Engagement (CIRCLE).

López, Mark Hugo, Peter Levine, Deborah Both, Abby Kiesa, Emily Kirby, and Karlo Barrios Marcelo. 2006. *The 2006 Civic and Political Health of the Nation: A Detailed Look at How Youth Participate in Politics and Communities*. College Park, Md.: University of Maryland, School of Public Policy, Center for Information and Research on Civic Learning and Engagement (CIRCLE).

López, Mark Hugo, Karlo Barrios Marcelo, and Emily Hoban Kirby. 2007. *Youth Voter Turnout Increases in 2006*. College Park, Md.: University of Maryland, School of Public Policy, Center for Information and Research on Civic Learning and Engagement (CIRCLE).

Louie, Vivian, and Jennifer Holdaway. 2009. "Catholic Schools and Immigrant Students: A New Generation." *Teachers College Record* 111(3): 783–816.

Lucas, Samuel R. 1999. *Tracking Inequality: Stratification and Mobility in American High Schools*. New York: Teachers College Press.

Lucas, Samuel R., and Mark Berends. 2007. "Race and Track Location in U.S. Public Schools." *Research in Social Stratification and Mobility* 25(3): 169–87.

Mahoney, Kate S., and Jeff MacSwan. 2005. "Reexamining Identification and Reclassification of English Language Learners: A Critical Discussion of Select State Practices." *Bilingual Research Journal* 29(1): 31–42.

Marri, Anand. 2005. "Building a Framework for Classroom-Based Multicultural Democratic Education: Learning from Three Skilled Teachers." *Teachers College Record* 107(5): 1036–59.

Marsh, Herbert W. 1992. "Extracurricular Activities: Beneficial Extension of the Traditional Curriculum or Subversion of Academic Goals?" *Journal of Educational Psychology* 84(4): 553–62.

Marshall, T. H. 1950. *Citizenship and Social Class*. Cambridge: Cambridge University Press.

Massey, Douglas S., and Chiara Capoferro. 2008. "The Geographic Diversification of American Immigration." In *New Faces in New Places*, edited by Douglas S. Massey. New York: Russell Sage Foundation.

McFarland, Daniel A., and Reuben J. Thomas. 2006. "Bowling Young: How Youth Voluntary Associations Influence Adult Political Participation." *American Sociological Review* 71(3): 401–25.

McGroarty, Mary. 2002. "Evolving Influences on Educational Language Policies." In *Language Policies in Education: Critical Issues*, edited by James W. Tollefson. Portsmouth, N.H.: Routledge.

McNeal, Ralph B., Jr. 1999. "Parent Involvement as Social Capital: Differential Effectiveness on Science Achievement, Truancy, and Dropping Out." *Social Forces* 78(1): 117–44.

Mertz, Elizabeth. 1982. "Language and Mind: A Whorfian Folk Theory in United States Language Law." Austin, Tex.: Southwest Educational Development Laboratory.

Millard, Ann V., and Jorge Chapa. 2004. *Apple Pie and Enchiladas: Latino Newcomers in the Rural Midwest.* Austin: University of Texas Press.

Miller, Warren E., and J. Merrill Shanks. 1996. *The New American Voter.* Cambridge, Mass.: Harvard University Press.

Milligan, Kevin, Enrico Morettib, and Philip Oreopoulosc. 2004. "Does Education Improve Citizenship? Evidence from the United States and the United Kingdom." *Journal of Public Economics* 88(9–10): 1667–95.

Minicucci, Catherine, and Laurie Olsen. 1992. *Programs for Secondary Limited English Proficient Students: A California Study.* Washington, D.C.: National Clearinghouse for Bilingual Education.

———. 1993. "Caught Unawares: California Secondary Schools Confront the Immigrant Student Challenge." *Multicultural Education* 1(2): 16–19.

Muller, Chandra. 1993. "Parent Involvement and Academic Achievement: An Analysis of Family Resources Available to the Child." In *Parents, Their Children, and Schools,* edited by Barbara Schneider and James S. Coleman. Boulder, Colo.: Westview.

Muller, Chandra, Jennifer Pearson, Catherine Riegle-Crumb, Jennifer Harris-Requejo, Kathryn S. Schiller, R. Kelly Raley, Amy G. Langenkamp, Sarah Crissey, Anna S. Mueller, Rebecca M. Callahan, Lindsey Wilkinson, and Samuel H. Field. 2007. *Wave III Education Data: Design and Implementation of the Adolescent Health and Academic Achievement Study.* Chapel Hill, N.C.: Carolina Population Center, University of North Carolina at Chapel Hill.

Muller, Chandra, Catherine Riegle-Crumb, Kathryn S. Schiller, Lindsey Wilkinson, and Kenneth A. Frank. 2010. "Race and Academic Achievement in Racially Diverse High Schools: Opportunity and Stratification." *Teachers College Record* 112(4): 1038–63.

National Association of Secretaries of State. 2000. "American Youth Attitudes on Politics, Citizenship, Government, and Voting." Lexington, Ky.: National Association of Secretaries of State.

National Center for Education Statistics, Schools and Staffing Survey, 1999–2000. Washington, D.C.: U.S. Department of Education.

National Education Association. 2004. "No Subject Left Behind? Think Again." *NEA Today* 23(3): 26–27.

Nation's Report Card. 2010. "Civics 2010." Washington: National Center for Education Statistics, Institute of Education Sciences.

Nelson, Jack L. 2001. "Defining Social Studies." In *Critical Issues in Social Studies Research for the Twenty-First Century,* edited by William B. Stanley. Greenwich, Conn.: Information Age Publishing.

Newmann, Fred M., Helen M. Marks, and Adam Gamoran. 1996. "Authentic Pedagogy and Student Performance." *American Journal of Education* 104(4): 280–312.

Newstreet, Carmen. 2008. "Paul Revere Rides Through High School Government Class: Teacher Research and the Power of Discussion to Motivate Thinking." *The Social Studies* 99(1): 9–12.

Nie, Norman H., Jane Junn, and Kenneth Stehlik-Barry. 1996. *Education and Democratic Citizenship in America.* Chicago: University of Chicago Press.

Niemi, Richard G., Mary A. Hepburn, and Chris Chapman. 2000. "Community Service by High School Students: A Cure for Civic Ills." *Political Behavior* 22(1): 45–69.

Niemi, Richard G., and Jane Junn. 1998. *Civic Education: What Makes Students Learn.* New Haven, Conn.: Yale University Press.

Niemi, Richard G., and Julia Smith. 2001. "Enrollments in High School Government Classes: Are We Shortchanging Both Citizenship and Political Science Training?" *PS: Political Science and Politics* 34(2): 281–87.

Oakes, Jeannie. 1985. *Keeping Track: How Schools Structure Inequality.* New Haven, Conn.: Yale University Press.

Olsen, Laurie. 1995. "School Restructuring and the Needs of Immigrant Students." In *California's Immigrant Children: Theory, Research, and Implications for Educational Policy,* edited by Rubén G. Rumbaut and Wayne A. Cornelius. San Diego: University of California, Center for U.S.-Mexican Studies.

———. 1997. *Made in America: Immigrant Students in Our Public Schools.* New York: New Press.

———. 2000. "Learning English and Learning America: Immigrants in the Center of a Storm." *Theory into Practice* 39(4): 196–202.

———. 2010. *Reparable Harm: Fulfilling the Unkept Promise of Educational Opportunity for California's Long-Term English Learners.* Long Beach: Californians Together.

Orfield, Gary. 2001. *Schools More Separate: Consequences of a Decade of Resegregation—New Research Findings.* Cambridge, Mass.: Harvard University Press.

Pantoja, Adrian D., Ricardo Ramirez, and Gary M. Segura. 2001. "Citizens by Choice, Voters by Necessity: Patterns in Political Mobilization by Naturalized Latinos." *Political Research Quarterly* 54(4): 729–50.

Parker, Walter C. 2001a. "Educating Democratic Citizens: A Broad View." *Theory into Practice* 40(1): 6–14.

———. 2001b. "Toward Enlightened Political Engagement." In *Critical Issues in Social Studies Research for the Twenty-First Century,* edited by William B. Stanley. Greenwich, Conn.: Information Age Publishing.

———. 2005. "Teaching Against Idiocy." *Phi Delta Kappan* 86(5): 344–51.

———. 2010. "Listening to Strangers: Classroom Discussion in Democratic Education." *Teachers College Record* 112(11): 2815–32.

Passel, Jeffrey S. 2011. "Demography of Immigrant Youth: Past, Present, and Future." *The Future of Children* 21(1): 19–41.

Passel, Jeffrey S., and D'Vera Cohn. 2008. *U.S. Population Projections: 2005–2050.* Washington, D.C.: Pew Research Center.

Passel, Jeffrey S., and Paul Taylor. 2010. "Unauthorized Immigrants and Their U.S.-Born Children." Washington, D.C.: Pew Hispanic Center.

Pavlenko, Aneta. 2002. "'We Have Room for But One Language Here': Language and National Identity in the U.S. at the Turn of the Twentieth Century." *Multilingua* 21(2/3): 163–96.

Perreira, Krista M., Kathleen Mullan Harris, and Lee Dohoon. 2006. "Making It in America: High School Completion by Immigrant and Native Youth." *Demography* 43(3): 511–36.

Pew Hispanic Center. 2009. *Statistical Portrait of the Foreign-Born Population in the United States, 2007.* Washington, D.C.: Pew Research Center.

Phelan, Patricia, Hanh Cao Yu, and Ann Locke Davidson. 1994. "Navigating the Psychosocial Pressures of Adolescence: The Voices and Experiences of High School Youth." *American Educational Research Journal* 31(2): 415–47.

Plotke, David. 1999. "Immigration and Political Incorporation in the Contemporary United States." In *The Handbook of International Migration: The American Experience,* edited by Charles Hirschman, Philip Kasinitz, and Josh DeWind. New York: Russell Sage Foundation.

Pong, Suet-ling, and Lingxin Hao. 2007. "Neighborhood and School Factors in the School Performance of Immigrants' Children." *International Migration Review* 41(1): 206–41.

Portes, Alejandro. 2002. "English-Only Triumphs, but the Costs Are High." *Contexts* 1(1): 1–6.

Portes, Alejandro, and A. Allepick. 1993. *City on the Edge: The Transformation of Miami.* Berkeley: University of California Press.

Portes, Alejandro, and Patricia Fernandez-Kelly. 2008. "No Margin for Error: Educational and Occupational Achievement Among Disadvantaged Children of Immigrants." *Annals of the American Academy of Political and Social Science* 620(1): 12–36.

Portes, Alejandro, and Lingxin Hao. 1998. "E Pluribus Unum: Bilingualism and Loss of Language in the Second Generation." *Sociology of Education* 71(4): 269–94.

———. 2004. "The Schooling of Children of Immigrants: Contextual Effects on the Educational Attainment of the Second Generation." *Proceedings of the National Academy of Sciences of the United States of America* 101(33): 11920–27.

Portes, Alejandro, and Dag MacLeod. 1996. "Educational Progress of Children of Immigrants: The Roles of Class, Ethnicity, and School Context." *Sociology of Education* 69(4): 255–75.

Portes, Alejandro, and Rubén G. Rumbaut. 2001. *Legacies: The Story of the Immigrant Second Generation.* Berkeley: University of California Press.

———. 2006. *Immigrant America: A Portrait.* Berkeley: University of California Press.

Portes, Alejandro, and Min Zhou. 1993. "The New Second Generation: Segmented Assimilation and Its Variants." *Annals of the American Academy of Political and Social Sciences* 530(1): 74–96.

Putnam, Robert D. 2000. *Bowling Alone: The Collapse and Revival of American Community.* New York: Simon & Schuster.

Ragan, Alex, and Nonie Lesaux. 2006. "Federal, State, and District Level English

Language Learner Program Entry and Exit Requirements: Effects on the Education of Language Minority Students." In *Education Policy Analysis Archives* 14(August). Available at: http://epaa.asu.edu/ojs/article/view/91. Accessed December 31, 2012.

Ramakrishnan, S. Karthick. 2005. *Democracy in Immigrant America: Changing Demographics and Political Participation.* Stanford, Calif.: Stanford University Press.

Ramakrishnan, S. Karthick, and Irene Bloemraad. 2008. *Civic Hopes and Political Realities: Immigrants, Community Organizations, and Political Engagement.* New York: Russell Sage Foundation.

Ramakrishnan, S. Karthick, and Thomas J. Espenshade. 2001. "Immigrant Incorporation and Political Participation in the United States." *International Migration Review* 35(3): 870–909.

Ravitch, Diane. 2010. *The Death and Life of the Great American School System.* New York: Basic Books.

Riegle-Crumb, Catherine. 2006. "The Path Through Math: Course Sequences and Academic Performance at the Intersection of Race-Ethnicity and Gender." *American Journal of Education* 113(1): 101–22.

———. 2010. "More Girls Go to College: Exploring the Social and Academic Factors Behind the Female Postsecondary Advantage Among Hispanic and White Students." *Research in Higher Education* 51(6): 573–93.

Rock, Tracy C., Tina Heafner, Katherine O'Connor, Jeff Passe, Sandra Oldendorf, Amy Good, and Sandra Byrd. 2006. "One State Closer to a National Crisis: A Report on Elementary Social Studies Education in North Carolina Schools." *Theory and Research in Social Education* 34(4): 455–83.

Rodríguez, Tomas D. 2003. "School Social Context Effects on Gender Differences in Academic Achievement Among Second-Generation Latinos." *Journal of Hispanic Higher Education* 2(1): 30–45.

Rosenbaum, Emily, and Jessie Anne Rochford. 2008. "Generational Patterns in Academic Performance: The Variable Effects of Attitudes and Social Capital." *Social Science Research* 37(1): 350–72.

Ross, E. Wayne. 1997. "The Struggle for the Social Studies Curriculum." In *The Social Studies Curriculum: Purposes, Problems, and Possibilities,* edited by E. Wayne Ross. Albany, N.Y.: State University of New York Press.

Rothschild, Eric. 1999. "Four Decades of the Advanced Placement Program." *The History Teacher* 32(2): 175–206.

Ruiz-de-Velasco, Jorge, and Michael Fix. 2000. *Overlooked and Underserved: Immigrant Students in U.S. Secondary Schools.* Washington, D.C.: Urban Institute.

Rumbaut, Rubén G. 1994. "The Crucible Within: Ethnic Identity, Self-Esteem, and Segmented Assimilation Among Children of Immigrants." *International Migration Review* 28(4 Special Issue): 748–94.

Rumbaut, Rubén G., and Alejandro Portes. 2001. *Ethnicities: Children of Immigrants in America.* Berkeley: University of California Press.

Sanders, Jimy M., and Victor Nee. 1996. "Immigrant Self-Employment: The Family as Social Capital and the Value of Human Capital." *American Sociological Review* 61(2): 231–49.

Saxe, David Warren. 1992. "Framing a Theory for Social Studies Foundations." *Review of Educational Research* 62(3): 259–77.

Schildkraut, Deborah J. 2003. "American Identity and Attitudes Toward Official-English Policies." *Political Psychology* 24(3): 469–99.

Schiller, Kathryn S., and Chandra Muller. 2003. "Raising the Bar and Equity? Effects of State High School Graduation Requirements and Accountability Policies on Students' Mathematics Course Taking." *Educational Evaluation and Policy Studies* 25(3): 299–318.

Schmid, Carol. 2001. "Educational Achievement, Language-Minority Students, and the New Second Generation." *Sociology of Education* 74 (extra issue): 71–87.

Schwartz, Amy Ellen, and Leanna Steifel. 2004. "Immigrants and the Distribution of Resources Within an Urban School District." *Educational Evaluation and Policy Analysis* 26(4): 303–27.

Seif, Hinda. 2011. "'Unapologetic and Unafraid': Immigrant Youth Come Out from the Shadows." *New Directions for Child and Adolescent Development* No. 134: 59–75.

Seixas, Peter. 1993. "Historical Understanding Among Adolescents in a Multicultural Setting." *Curriculum Inquiry* 23(3): 301–27.

Shea, Daniel M., and John C. Green. 2007. "The Turned-Off Generation: Fact or Fiction?" In *Fountain of Youth: Strategies and Tactics for Mobilizing America's Young Voters,* edited by Daniel M. Shea and John C. Green. New York: Rowman and Littlefield.

Sherrod, Lonnie R. 2003. "Promoting the Development of Citizenship in Diverse Youth." *PS: Political Science and Politics* 36(2): 287–92.

Sherrod, Lonnie R., Constance Flanagan, and James Youniss. 2002. "Dimensions of Citizenship and Opportunities for Youth Development: The What, Why, When, Where, and Who of Citizenship Development." *Applied Developmental Science* 6(4): 264–72.

Smith, Elizabeth S. 1999. "The Effects of Investments in the Social Capital of Youth on Political and Civic Behavior in Young Adulthood: A Longitudinal Analysis." *Political Psychology* 20(3): 553–80.

Stanton-Salazar, Ricardo D., and Sanford M. Dornbusch. 1995. "Social Capital and the Reproduction of Inequality: Information Networks Among Mexican-Origin High School Students." *Sociology of Education* 68(2): 116–35.

Stepick, Alex, and Carol Dutton-Stepick. 2002. "Becoming American, Constructing Ethnicity: Immigrant Youth and Civic Engagement." *Applied Developmental Science* 6(4): 246–57.

Stevenson, David Lee, Kathryn S. Schiller, and Barbara Schneider. 1994. "Sequences of Opportunities for Learning." *Sociology of Education* 67(3): 184–98.

Stone, Susan, and Meekyung Han. 2005. "Perceived School Environments, Perceived Discrimination, and School Performance Among Children of Mexican Immigrants." *Children and Youth Services Review* 27(1): 51–66.

Suárez-Orozco, Marcelo M., Carola Suárez-Orozco, and Irina Todorova. 2008. *Learning a New Land: Immigrant Students in American Society.* Cambridge, Mass.: Harvard University Press.

Suro, Robert. 2005. "Latino Power? It Will Take Time for the Population Boom to Translate." *Washington Post,* June 27, 2005.

Tate, William F. 1997. "Race-Ethnicity, SES, Gender, and Language Proficiency Trends in Mathematics Achievement: An Update." *Journal for Research in Mathematics Education* 28(6): 652–79.

ten Dam, Geert, and Monique Volman. 2004. "Critical Thinking as a Citizenship Competence: Teaching Strategies." *Learning and Instruction* 14(4): 359–79.

Thornton, Stephen J. 1994. "The Social Studies Near Century's End: Reconsidering Patterns of Curriculum and Instruction." *Review of Research in Education* 20: 223–54.

Tienda, Marta, and Ron Haskins. 2011. "Immigrant Children: Introducing the Issue." *The Future of Children* 21(1): 1–18.

Torney-Purta, Judith. 2002. "The School's Role in Developing Civic Engagement: A Study of Adolescents in Twenty-Eight Countries." *Applied Developmental Science* 6(4): 203–12.

Torney-Purta, Judith, Carolyn H. Barber, and Britt Wilkenfeld. 2006. "Differences in the Civic Knowledge and Attitudes of Adolescents in the United States by Immigrant Status and Hispanic Background." *Prospects* 36(3): 343–54.

Torney-Purta, Judith, Rainer Lehmann, Hans Oswald, and Wolfram Schulz. 2001. "Citizenship and Education in Twenty-Eight Countries: Civic Knowledge and Engagement at Age Fourteen." Amsterdam: International Association for the Evaluation of Educational Achievement (IEA).

Torney-Purta, Judith, Wendy Klandl Richardson, and Carolyn Barber. 2004. "Trust in Government-Related Institutions and Civic Engagement Among Adolescents: Analysis of Five Countries from the IEA Civic Education Study." College Park: University of Maryland, School of Public Policy, Center for Information and Research on Civic Learning and Engagement (CIRCLE).

Tyack, David B. 1974. *The One Best System: A History of American Urban Education.* Cambridge, Mass.: Harvard University Press.

———. 2003. *Seeking Common Ground: Public Schools in a Diverse Society.* Cambridge, Mass.: Harvard University Press.

Urban Institute. 2002. *Immigrant Families and Workers.* Washington, D.C.: Urban Institute.

———. 2006. *Children of Immigrants: Facts and Figures.* Washington, D.C.: Urban Institute.

U.S. Census Bureau. 2006. "Hispanics in the United States." Washington, D.C.: U.S. Census Bureau, Ethnicity and Ancestry Branch, Population Division.

U.S. Census Bureau and Department of Education. 1990. Census 1990. National Center for Education Statistics, School District Demographics System. Washington, D.C.: U.S. Department of Commerce.

U.S. Census Bureau and Department of Education. 2006–2008. American Community Survey United States, 2006–2008. National Center for Education Statistics, School District Demographics System. Washington, D.C.: U.S. Department of Commerce.

U.S. Department of Education. 2001. *No Child Left Behind Act of 2001* (NCLB). Washington, D.C.: U.S. Department of Education.

Valdés, Guadalupe. 1996. *Con Respeto—Bridging the Distances Between Culturally Diverse Families and Schools: An Ethnographic Portrait.* New York: Teachers College Press.

Valenzuela, Angela. 1999. *Subtractive Schooling: U.S.-Mexican Youth and the Politics of Caring.* Albany: State University of New York Press.

Vandevoort, Leslie G., and David C. Berliner. 2004. "National Board Certified Teachers and Their Students' Achievement." *Education Policy Analysis Archives* 12(46): 1–117.

VanFossen, Phillip J. 2005. "'Reading and Math Take So Much of the Time . . .': An Overview of Social Studies Instruction in Elementary Classrooms in Indiana." *Theory and Research in Social Education* 33(3): 376–403.

Verba, Sidney, Kay Lehman Schlozman, and Henry E. Brady. 1995. *Voice and Equality: Civic Voluntarism in American Politics.* Cambridge, Mass.: Harvard University Press.

———. 1996. *Voice and Equality: Civic Volunteerism in American Politics.* Cambridge, Mass.: Harvard Univesity Press.

Vigil, James Diego, and Steve Chong Yun. 1998. "Vietnamese Youth Gangs in the Context of Multiple Marginality and the Los Angeles Youth Gang Phenomenon." In *Gangs and Youth Subcultures: International Explorations,* edited by Kayleen M. Hazlehurst and Cameron Hazlehurst. New Brunswick, N.J.: Transaction Publishers.

Vincent, Ryan S. 2004–2005. "No Child Left Behind, Only the Arts and Humanities: Emerging Inequalities in Education Fifty Years After *Brown.*" *Washburn Law Journal* 44(1): 127–56.

Warikoo, Natasha, and Prudence Carter. 2009. "Cultural Explanations for Racial and Ethnic Stratification in Academic Achievement: A Call for a New and Improved Theory." *Review of Educational Research* 79(1): 366–94.

Waters, Mary C., and Tomás R. Jiménez. 2005. "Assessing Immigrant Assimilation: New Empirical and Theoretical Challenges." *Annual Review of Sociology* 31(1): 105–25.

White, Michael, and Jennifer Glick. 2000. "Generation Status, Social Capital, and the Routes Out of High School." *Sociological Forum* 15(4): 671–91.

Wiley, Terrence G. 2007. "Accessing Language Rights in Education: A Brief History of the U.S. Context." In *Bilingual Education: An Introductory Reader (Bilingual Education and Bilingualism),* edited by Ofelia García and Colin Baker. Clevedon, U.K.: Multilingual Matters LTD.

Wiley, Terrence G., and Wayne E. Wright. 2004. "Against the Undertow: Language-Minority Education Policy and Politics in the 'Age of Accountability.'" *Educational Policy* 18(1): 142–68.

Wilkerson, Miranda E., and Joseph Salmons. 2008. "'Good Old Immigrants of Yesteryear' Who Didn't Learn English: Germans in Wisconsin." *American Speech* 83(3): 259–83.

Wong, Janelle S. 2000. "The Effects of Age and Political Exposure on the Development of Party Identification Among Asian American and Latino Immigrants in the United States." *Political Behavior* 22(4): 341–71.

Wong, Janelle, and Vivian Tseng. 2007. "Political Socialisation in Immigrant Families: Challenging Top-Down Parental Socialisation Models." *Journal of Ethnic and Migration Studies* 34(1): 151–68.

Wortham, Stanton, Enrique Murillo, and Edmund T. Hamann. 2002. *Education in the New Latino Diaspora: Policy and the Politics of Identity.* Westport, Conn.: Ablex Publishing.

Wuthnow, Robert. 1997. *The Changing Character of Social Capital in the United States.* Princeton, N.J.: Princeton University, Department of Sociology.

Youniss, James, Susan Bales, Verona Christmas-Best, Marcelo Diversi, Milbrey McLaughlin, and Rainer Silbereisen. 2002. "Youth Civic Engagement in the Twenty-First Century." *Journal of Research on Adolescence* 12(1): 121–48.

Youniss, James, Jeffrey A. McLellan, and Miranda Yates. 1997. "What We Know About Engendering Civic Identity." *American Behavioral Scientist* 40(5): 620–31.

Zaff, Jonathan F., Kristin A. Moore, Angela Romano Papillo, and Stephanie Williams. 2003. "Implications of Extracurricular Activity Participation During Adolescence on Positive Outcomes." *Journal of Adolescent Research* 18(16): 599–630.

Zehler, Annette, Howard L. Fleischman, Paul J. Hopstock, Michael L. Pendzick, Todd G. Stephenson, and S. Sapru. 2003. "Descriptive Study of Services to LEP Students and LEP Students with Disabilities." Special Topic Report 4, submitted to the U.S. Department of Education. Arlington, Va.: Development Associates, Inc. Available at: http://www.ncela.gwu.edu/files/rcd/BE021199/special_ed4.pdf. Accessed December 31, 2012.

Zhou, Min. 1997a. "Growing Up American: The Challenge Confronting Immigrant Children and Children of Immigrants." *Annual Review of Sociology* 23: 63–95.

———. 1997b. "Segmented Assimilation: Issues, Controversies, and Recent Research on the New Second Generation." *International Migration Review* 31(4): 975–1008.

———. 2009. "How Neighborhoods Matter for Immigrant Children: The Formation of Educational Resources in Chinatown, Koreatown, and Pico Union, Los Angeles." *Journal of Ethnic and Migration Studies* 35(7): 1153–79.

Zhou, Min, and Susan S. Kim. 2006. "Community Forces, Social Capital, and Educational Achievement: The Case of Supplementary Education in the Chinese and Korean Immigrant Communities." *Harvard Educational Review* 76(1): 1–29.

Zukin, Cliff, Scott Keeter, Molly Andolina, Krista Jenkins, and Michael X. Delli Carpini. 2006. *A New Engagement? Political Participation, Civil Life, and the Changing American Citizen.* Oxford: Oxford University Press.

Zuniga, Keren, Joanne K. Olson, and Mary Winter. 2005. "Science Education for Rural Latino/a Students: Course Placement and Success in Science." *Journal of Research in Science Teaching* 42(4): 376–402.

INDEX

Boldface numbers refer to figures and tables

Abdi, Cawo, 144*n*1(ch5)

academic achievement and preparation, 62–77; and course-taking, 65–68, 77; credit completion, 93–95; data sources, 10; English language proficiency issues, 69–76; and extracurricular activity participation, 39; grades, 4, 64–65, 68, 75, 93, 99, 115; high schools' role, 128–29; by immigrant status and other background characteristics, 68–69, **70–71,** 93–95; introduction, 62–63; opportunities to learn, 63–64; and political participation, 40–41, 42; racial-ethnic gap, 92; test scores, 64–65

academic clubs, 55, 56

academic courses. *See* course-taking

academic orientation or emphasis, 59–61, 101

academic stratification: curriculum differences, 101; family background effects, 99; impact of, 36–37, 62, 92, 126; and language proficiency, 69–76; mathematics, 98; racial-ethnic differences, 92; and social science coursework, 99–100; tracking, 63–64, 68–76, 79

accountability, school, 2, 4–5, 98–99, 123

ACS (American Community Survey), 18

Add Health. *See* National Longitudinal Study of Adolescent Health (Add Health)

Adolescent Health and Academic Achievement Study (AHAA), 9–10, 93, 133–34

adolescents, forces shaping transition to adulthood, 33–44. *See also* families and family background; high schools

Advanced Placement (AP), 44, 65, 80

Afghanistan, War in, 26

African Americans. *See* Black Americans

age differences, in political participation, 31

agency, 92

AHAA (Adolescent Health and Academic Achievement Study), 9–10, 93, 133–34

AH-PVT verbal scores, 102, **103,** 105, 137

Alabama: immigrant population, 15

American Community Survey (ACS), 18